GIFTED GAMES™

COGAT® TEST PREP • LEVEL 8

Revised Edition With Updated Introduction & 300 Questions

Gateway Gifted Resources™
www.GatewayGifted.com

PLEASE LEAVE US
A REVIEW!

Thank you for selecting this book. We are a family-owned publishing company - a consortium of educators, test designers, book designers, parents, and kid-testers.

We would be thrilled if you left us a quick review on the website where you purchased this book!

The Gateway Gifted Resources™ Team
www.GatewayGifted.com

TABLE OF CONTENTS

INTRODUCTION

WORKBOOK

PRACTICE QUESTION SET

ANSWER KEYS & DIRECTIONS

ABOUT THE COGAT® LEVEL 8: The COGAT® (Cognitive Abilities Test®) Level 8 is given to children in second grade. As the name suggests, it assesses your child's cognitive skills. The test is divided into 3 "batteries." Each of the batteries has 3 question types. The Verbal Battery's question types are Picture Analogies, Picture Classification, and Sentence Completion. The Non-Verbal Battery's question types are Figure Analogies, Figure Classification, and Paper Folding. The Quantitative Battery's question types are Number Analogies, Number Puzzles, and Number Series. Each question type has 18 questions, except for Paper Folding and Number Puzzles, which have 14 questions each. The test has 154 questions total. The test, about two hours in length, is administered in different testing sessions. Children are not expected to complete 154 questions in one session. **See p.6-9 for more on these question types.**

ABOUT COGAT® TESTING PROCEDURES: These vary by school. Tests may be given individually or in a group. These tests may be used as the single factor for admission to gifted programs, or they may be used in combination with IQ tests or as part of a student "portfolio." They are used by some schools together with tests like Iowa Assessments™ to measure academic achievement. Check with your testing site to determine its specific testing procedures.

ABOUT THIS BOOK: This book introduces cognitive skill-building exercises to early elementary-age children through child-friendly subjects. The format is designed to help prepare children taking standardized multiple-choice gifted and talented assessment tests like the COGAT®. This book has five parts.

1. Introduction (p.4-9): About the COGAT® and about this book (p.4); Test Taking Tips (p.5), The Gifted Detective Agency (p.5), and Question Examples & Explanations (p.6-9).

2. Workbook (p.10-44): Pages 10-44 are designed similarly to content tested in the COGAT®'s nine test question types. The Workbook exercises are meant to be done together with no time limit. **Before doing the Workbook with your child, read the Question Examples & Explanations (p.6-9).**

3. Practice Question Set (p.46-87): The Practice Question Set helps children develop critical thinking and test-taking skills. A "score" (a percentile rank) cannot be obtained from this. (See below for more on gifted test scoring.) It provides an introduction to standardized test-taking in a relaxed manner (parents may provide guidance if needed). It is an opportunity for children to practice focusing on a group of questions for a longer time period (something to which some children are not accustomed). It is also a way for parents to identify points of strength/ weakness in COGAT® question types. It is divided into three sections to mirror the three COGAT® batteries: Verbal, Quantitative, and Non-Verbal.

4. Directions and Answer Keys (p.88-93): These pages contain answer keys for both the Workbook and the Practice Question Set. They also include the directions to read to your child for the Practice Question Set. (To mimic actual tests, the directions are separate from the child's pages in the Practice Question Set.)

5. Afterword (p.94): Information on additional books, free eBook of practice questions, and your child's certificate

QUESTION NOTE: Because each child has different cognitive abilities, the questions in this book are at varied skill levels. The exercises may or may not require a great deal of parental guidance to complete, depending on your child's abilities and familiarity with this multiple choice question format. Most sections of the Workbook begin with a relatively easy question. We suggest always completing at least the first question together, ensuring your child is not confused about what the question asks or with the directions.

"BUBBLES" NOTE: Your child will most likely have to fill in "bubbles" (the circles) to indicate answer choices. (Check with your testing site regarding its "bubble" use.) Show your child how to fill in the bubble to indicate his/her answer choice using a pencil. If your child needs to change his/her answer, (s)he should erase the original mark and fill in the new choice.

SCORING NOTE: Check with your school/program for its specific scoring and admissions requirements. Here is a general summary of the scoring process. First, your child's raw score is established. This is the number of questions correctly answered. Points are not deducted for questions answered incorrectly. Next, this score is compared to other test-takers of his/her same age group (and, for the COGAT®, the same grade level) using various indices to then calculate your child's stanine (a score from one to nine) and percentile rank. If your child achieved the percentile rank of 98%, then (s)he scored as well as or better than 98% of test-takers. In general, gifted programs accept scores of *at least* 98% or *higher*. Please note that a percentile rank "score" cannot be obtained from our practice material. This material has not been given to a large enough sample of test-takers to develop any kind of base score necessary for percentile rank calculations.

TEST TAKING TIPS
• Have your child practice listening carefully. Paying attention is important, because test questions are not repeated.
• In the Workbook section, go through the exercises together by talking about them: what the exercise is asking the child to do and what makes the answer choices correct/incorrect. This will not only familiarize your child with working through exercises, it will also help him/her develop a process of elimination (getting rid of any answer choices that are incorrect).
• Make sure your child looks at **each** answer choice.
• Test-takers receive points for the number of correct answers. If your child says that (s)he does not know the answer, (s)he should first eliminate any answers that are obviously not correct. Guess instead of leaving a question unanswered.
• Remind your child to choose only ONE answer.
• Remember common sense tips like getting enough sleep. It has been scientifically proven that kids perform below their grade level when they are tired. Feed them a breakfast for sustained energy and concentration (complex carbohydrates and protein; avoid foods/drinks high in sugar). Have them use the restroom prior to the test.

THE "GIFTED DETECTIVE AGENCY"
To increase engagement and to add an incentive to complete exercises, a detective theme accompanies this book. The book's characters belong to a detective agency. They want your child to help them solve "puzzles" so that your child can join, too! As your child completes the book, allow him/her to "check" the boxes at the bottom of the Workbook and Practice Question Set pages. If your child "checks all the boxes," (s)he will "join." Feel free to modify the number of pages/ exercises your child must complete in order to receive his/her certificate (p. 95).

The Gifted Detective Agency

We're the Gifted Detective Agency. We need another member, and we think YOU have what it takes to join us.

Detectives in the Gifted Detective Agency figure out puzzles and find answers to questions.

To prove you're ready to join us, you'll put your skills to the test in this book. Together with your mom, dad, or other adult, you need to solve puzzles. The adult helping you will explain what to do - listen carefully!

A good detective:
• Pays attention and listens closely
• Looks carefully at all choices before answering a question
• Keeps trying even if some questions are hard

After finishing each page, mark the box at the bottom. Like this:

Your parent (or other adult) will tell you which pages to do. After finishing them all, you will become a member of the Gifted Detective Agency! (Remember, it's more important to answer the questions the right way than to try to finish them really fast.) After you're done, you'll get your very own Gifted Detective Agency certificate.

When you're ready to start the puzzles, write your name here: _____

QUESTION EXAMPLES & EXPLANATIONS This section introduces the 9 COGAT® question types through <u>basic</u> examples and explanations. In each question type (#1-#9), show your child the example (one basic example question consisting of images), then read the directions aloud. After the directions there are additional explanations for parents.

VERBAL BATTERY

<u>1. Picture Analogies</u> Directions: The pictures in the top boxes go together in some way. Look at the bottom boxes. One is empty. Next to the boxes is a row of pictures. Which one goes with the picture in the bottom box like the pictures in the top boxes do?

Explanation Your child must determine how the top set is related. Then, (s)he must determine what answer choice goes in the box with a question mark so that the bottom set has the same relationship as the top. It's helpful to come up with a "rule" describing how the top set goes together. Take this rule, apply it to the bottom picture and determine which answer choice makes the bottom set follow the same "rule." If more than one choice works, then you need a more specific rule.

Here is a tire and a car. A tire is part of a car. A tire is found on a car. A rule would be, "the thing in the first box is found on the thing in the second box. The first thing is part of the second thing." On the bottom is a leaf. Try the answer choices with the rule. An acorn is not correct because a leaf is not part of an acorn, nor is a leaf found on a grasshopper, nor on the sun. A tree is correct because a leaf is found on a tree. A leaf is part of a tree.

These simple examples are an introduction to common analogy logic. Read the "Question" then "Answer Choices" to your child. Which choice goes best? Note that all logic is *reversible*. For example, "Part: Whole" could also be "Whole: Part."

Analogy Logic	Questions	Answer Choices (Answer is Underlined)			
• "X": Opposite of "X"	On *is to* Off -as- Hot *is to* ?	Warm	Sun	<u>Cold</u>	Oven
• Part: Whole	Toe *is to* Foot -as- Petal *is to* ?	Stem	Bee	Leg	<u>Flower</u>
• Animal: Its Home	Bird *is to* Nest -as- Bat *is to* ?	<u>Cave</u>	Fly	Night	Wing
• Animal: Its Food	Seed *is to* Bird -as- Acorn *is to* ?	Nut	Peanut	<u>Squirrel</u>	Worm
• Animal: Its Covering	Bird *is to* Feathers -as- Fish *is to* ?	Swim	Sharks	Tails	<u>Scales</u>
• Baby: Adult	Duckling *is to* Duck -as- Chick *is to* ?	Goose	<u>Rooster</u>	Egg	Hatch
• Object: Item Used to Consume It	Soup *is to* Spoon -as- Drink *is to* ?	Liquid	Juice	Fork	<u>Straw</u>
• Vehicle: Worker	Police Car *is to* Police Officer -as- Spaceship *is to* ?	Rocket	Planet	<u>Astronaut</u>	Doctor
• Object: Location	Sun *is to* Sky -as- Swing *is to* ?	<u>Playground</u>	Monkey Bars	Fun	Up
• Similar: Similar	Turkey *is to* Parrot -as- Ant *is to* ?	Worm	<u>Beetle</u>	Duck	Crawl
• Food: Its Source	Honey *is to* Bee -as- Egg *is to* ?	Farm	Beehive	Round	<u>Chicken</u>
• Object: Creator	Painting *is to* Artist -as- Furniture *is to* ?	<u>Carpenter</u>	Tool	Chair	Potter
• Object: Container	Ice Cube *is to* Ice Tray -as- Flower *is to* ?	Petal	<u>Vase</u>	Smell	Florist
• Tool: Worker	Paintbrush *is to* Artist -as- Microscope *is to* ?	Telescope	<u>Scientist</u>	Lab	Fireman
• Object: Its Shape	Ball *is to* Sphere -as- Dice *is to* ?	Line	Oval	<u>Cube</u>	Cone
• Object: Action You Do When Using It	Microphone *is to* Talk -as- Binoculars *is to* ?	Hear	Speak	Spell	<u>See</u>
• Whole: Part (Materials to Make a Home)	Anthill *is to* Dirt -as- Cabin *is to* ?	<u>Wood</u>	House	Person	Sand
• Object: Location (Vehicles)	Jet *is to* Sky -as- Canoe *is to* ?	Boat	Land	<u>Water</u>	Sail
• Object: Where It's Used	Chalk *is to* Chalkboard -as- Paintbrush *is to* ?	Artist	<u>Easel</u>	Museum	Eraser

<u>2. Picture Classification</u> Directions: The top row shows pictures that are alike in some way. Look at the bottom row. Which bottom picture goes best with those on top?

Explanation Come up with a "rule" describing how they're alike. Then, see which answer choice follows the rule. If more than one choice does, then try a more specific rule.

Here are shoes, gloves, and dice. At first, it may be hard to see anything they have in common. Let's look closer. They each show a pair. This is how they are alike. The first and second pictures do not show a pair (a fan and bubble mix). The last choice, ice cream scoops, shows three scoops, not two. The third choice shows the correct answer – a pair of socks. Everyday life presents an opportunity to improve classification skills, as themes for Picture Classification (and Picture Analogies and Sentence Completion) include (but are not limited to) this list of common classification logic (gray font). Under the logic is an example question. Read the first list of 3 words to your child. Then, next to it, read the 4 choices to your child. Which one of the choices goes best with the first list?

- function and uses of common objects (i.e., writing and drawing / measuring / cutting / drinking / eating)
Fork / Chopsticks / Knife   Choices: Stove / Kitchen / Meat / <u>Spoon</u>   (Used For Eating)
- location of common objects
Refrigerator / Cabinet / Table   Choices: Bed / Restaurant / <u>Oven</u> / Shower   (Found In Kitchens)
- appearance of common objects (i.e., color; objects in pairs; objects with stripes vs. spots; object's shape)
Ketchup / Blood / Firetruck   Choices: <u>Cherry</u> / Mustard / Cucumber / Police car   (Red)
- characteristics of common objects (i.e., hot, cold)
Ice / Igloo / Popsicle   Choices: Cookie / <u>Snowman</u> / Palm Tree / Coffee   (Cold)
- animal/human homes
Aquarium / Barn / Nest   Choices: Feather / <u>Beehive</u> / Farmer / Fish   (Animal Homes)
- animal types
Leopard / Cheetah / Kitten   Choices: Elephant / Giraffe / <u>Tiger</u> / Bat   (Cats)
- natural habitats
Swamp / River / Pond   Choices: Desert / Mountain / House / <u>Ocean</u>   (Water)
- food types
Cake / Bread / Donut   Choices: Sherbet / <u>Cookie</u> / Syrup / Sugar   (Baked Foods)
- food growing location (i.e., on a tree, under the ground as a root, or on a vine)
Potato / Carrot / Onion   Choices: <u>Radish</u> / Melon / Pepper / Broccoli   (Root Vegetables)
- professions, community helpers
Doctor / Fireman / Vet   Choices: Witch / Wizard / <u>Teacher</u> / Baby   (Community Helpers)
- clothing (i.e., in what weather it's worn; on what body part it's worn)
Crown / Cowboy Hat / Cap   Choices: Necklace / <u>Helmet</u> / Gloves / Ring   (Worn On Head)
- transportation (i.e., where things travel, land/water/air; do they have wheels?)
Cruise Ship / Yacht / Kayak   Choices: <u>Canoe</u> / Fisherman / Dock / Jeep   (Travel On Water)

Additional topics include seasons and weather, sports objects, basic solar system knowledge (i.e., about the sun, moon, Earth), appearance of animal babies vs. adults, and musical instruments.

<u>3. Sentence Completion</u>   Directions: Listen to the question, then choose your answer. (Each question has different directions.) Max sees something floating in the water. Which one does Max see?

Explanation   The first choice, a rock, doesn't float, neither does a hammer or a coin. A beach ball does float in water; it is the answer. Your child must listen carefully. Test administrators will read the question only one time. To practice listening, remind your child to listen to **all** directions, from start to finish. Some kids stop paying attention when they think they know the answer. Build knowledge related to the list of themes in Picture Classification (which also helps with Picture Analogies).

NONVERBAL BATTERY

<u>4. Figure Analogies</u>   Directions: The pictures inside the top boxes go together in some way. Look at the bottom boxes. One is empty. Next to the boxes is a row of pictures. Which one goes with the picture in the bottom box like the pictures in the top boxes? (The word "picture" here actually refers to a "figure" that can consist of shapes, lines, etc.)

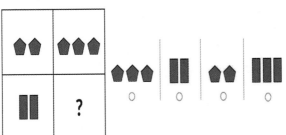

Explanation   Come up with a "rule" describing how the top set is related. This shows how the left box "changes" into the right box. On the left are 2 pentagons. On the right are 3 pentagons. The rule/change is that one more of the same kind of shape was added. On the bottom are 2 rectangles. The first choice is incorrect because it shows 3 pentagons - not the same shapes as the bottom box. The second choice is incorrect - it only shows 2 rectangles. The third choice is incorrect - it has 2 pentagons. The last choice is correct - there are 3 rectangles (1 more of the same shapes that were in the left box).

Here's a list of frequent "rules" / "changes" in Figure Analogies. Easier questions involve one "change," while more challenging questions involve more than one change (see example #9 below).

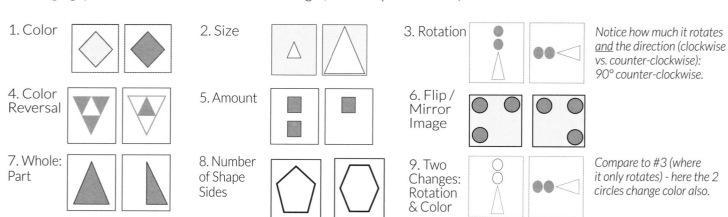

1. Color

2. Size

3. Rotation — *Notice how much it rotates and the direction (clockwise vs. counter-clockwise): 90° counter-clockwise.*

4. Color Reversal

5. Amount

6. Flip / Mirror Image

7. Whole: Part

8. Number of Shape Sides

9. Two Changes: Rotation & Color — *Compare to #3 (where it only rotates) - here the 2 circles change color also.*

<u>5. Figure Classification</u> **Directions:** Look at the top row of pictures. These pictures are alike in some way. Look at the bottom row. Which picture on the bottom goes best with the pictures on top?

Explanation The "pictures" in the directions refer to figures. Try to come up with a "rule" describing how the figures in the top row are alike. Then, see which choice follows the rule. If more than one choice would, then a more specific rule is needed. Here is 1 white triangle, 1 lightly shaded triangle, and 1 dark triangle. These are alike because they are all triangles. The first choice is correct because it's a triangle. None of the other choice (B, C, D) are triangles. If you get "stumped" by any of these, then try asking these kinds of questions:

• If there are 3 main figures (above), how many sides do they have?

• If there are 3 main figures, are they made of straight lines or are they rounded?

• If there are 3 main figures, are the shapes flat or 3-D?

• What direction are the figures facing?

• If the figures are different colors or if the figures have dots/lines inside, what do these look like?

• If the figures are divided, how are they divided?

• If each of the 3 figures is actually made of a group of shapes, how many shapes are in the group?

• If each of the 3 figures is actually made of a group of shapes, where are the shapes within the group?

• If each of the 3 figures is actually made of a group of shapes, is there a particular order of the group of shapes?

<u>6. Paper Folding</u> **Directions:** The top row of pictures shows a sheet of paper, how it was folded, and how something was cut out of it. Which picture on the bottom row shows how the paper would look after its unfolded?

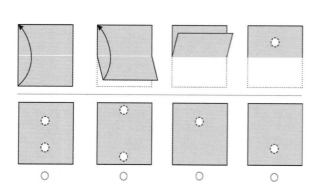

Explanation The first choice shows how it would look - 2 holes in the correct position. In the second choice, the holes are too close to the edge. In the third and fourth choice, there's only 1 hole. (Even though you only see 1 hole in the top row, when the paper is unfolded, there will be 2.) Here, holes have been cut out. However, other questions have different shapes cut out. Also, some questions will show paper that has been folded more than once.

Pay attention to: the number of objects cut out, where these objects are on the paper, and the direction they are facing. Try demonstrating with real paper. For example, you could do the first few Paper Folding questions (starting on p.28) using real paper and a hole puncher or scissors. Seeing real-life examples will assist children with correctly envisioning the paper folding steps during the test.

QUANTITATIVE BATTERY

7. Number Series Directions: Which rod would go in the place of the missing rod to finish the pattern?

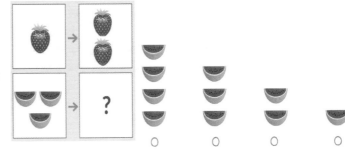

Explanation The last abacus rod is missing. Before it, the rods have made a pattern that your child must figure out. Then, "complete" the pattern with the correct answer choice. Young kids will frequently miscount the beads, so first, ensure they are correctly counting the beads. Looking across the abacus, from left to right, we see that with each rod the number of beads increases by 1. The rods go: 1–2–3–4–5–? This means that the missing rod needs 6 beads (Choice D).
Here is a list of common logic patterns found in Number Series questions. This book has examples of all of these.

Logic	Number of Beads	Logic	Number of Beads
1 bead is added	(0, 1, 2, 3, 4)	1 bead is taken away	(5, 4, 3, 2, 1)
2 beads are added	(0, 2, 4, 6, 8)	2 beads are taken away	(6, 4, 2, 0)
A-A-B-A-A-B	(3, 3, 2, 3, 3, 2)	A-B-C	(3, 2, 1, 3, 2, 1)
A-A-B-B-C-C	(3, 3, 2, 2, 1, 1)	A-B-C-zero-C-B-A	(6-3-2-0-2-3-6)

A / X / A+1 / X / A+2	(1, 0, 2, 0, 3, 0, 4) (here "X" is 0, it gets repeated every other time)
A / X / A-1 / X / A-2	(8, 1, 7, 1, 6, 1, 5) (here "X" is 1, it gets repeated every other time)
A / B / A+1 / B+1 / A+2 / B+2	(1, 5, 2, 6, 3, 7) (the first, third, fifth number & the second, fourth, sixth number increase by 1)
A / B / A-1 / B-1 / A-2 / B-2	(7, 3, 6, 2, 5, 1) (the first, third, fifth number & the second, fourth, sixth number decrease by 1)

8. Number Puzzles Directions: Look at the box that has the question mark. Which number would go here so that both of the sides of this equal sign (point to the equal sign) would have the same amount?

Two plus five equals seven. So, Choice C (5) is the correct answer.

Practice basic math equations together to build Number Puzzles skills.

7	=	2	+	?

3   4   5   6
○   ○   ○   ○

9. Number Analogies Directions: The pictures on top go together in some way. Look at the bottom boxes. One is empty. Next to the boxes is a row of pictures. Which choice goes with the bottom box like the pictures on top do?

Explanation Number Analogies are similar to Picture/Figure Analogies, but now the top set and the bottom set must have the same mathematical relationship. In the left box there is 1 object (a strawberry). In the right box there are 2 objects. From left to right, we see that 1 object has been added. So, the rule here is "1 is added" or "+1." In the bottom left box there are 3 objects. If our rule is "1 is added," when you have 3 and you add 1, you get 4. (3 + 1 = 4.) Choice A is the correct answer. Many of these questions involve addition and subtraction. However, some questions will involve dividing a group of objects (p.42 #6), as well as halving (p.41 #4), doubling (p.41 #3), tripling (p.44 #12), and dividing by 3 (p.42 #8).

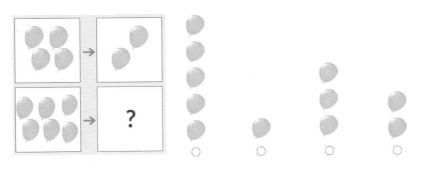

Tip: If you think a rule is to add or subtract on top, and find that none of the choices work with the bottom left box, then try to double or triple (if the top boxes increase from left to right) or halve or divide by 3 (if the top boxes decrease from left to right). On the left, from the top boxes, you may have come up with the rule "take away 2" (4 - 2 = 2). However, 6 - 2 = 4, but there is no answer choice with 4. In a case like this, try to halve (or divide by 3). Half of 4 equals 2. Half of 6 equals 3 (Choice C).

LET'S HELP ANYA FIGURE OUT WHAT GOES IN THE EMPTY BOX!

Directions: Look at these boxes that are on top. The pictures that are inside belong together in some way.

Then, look at these boxes that are on the bottom. One of these boxes on the bottom is empty.

Look next to the boxes. There is a row of pictures. Which one would go together with this picture that is in the bottom box like these pictures that are in the top boxes?

Parent note: Analogies compare sets of items, and the way they are related can easily be missed at first. Work through these together with your child so (s)he sees how the top set is related. Together, try to come up with a "rule" to describe how the top set is related. (The small arrows show that the pictures belong together in some way.) Then, look at the picture on the bottom. Take this "rule," use it together with the picture on the bottom, and figure out which of the answer choices would follow that same rule. For answer choices that do not follow this rule, eliminate them. If your child finds that more than one choice follows this rule, then try to come up with a rule that is more specific.

Example (read this to your child): Look at the boxes on top. In the first box there is a tiger. In the second box there is a lion. (Talk about the two pictures and try to come up with a "rule.") A tiger is a type of cat. A lion is a type of cat. What is in the bottom box? It is an ant. Now, let's look at the answer choices. Which one goes with the picture of the ant in the same way that the pictures in the top row go together?

The beetle. An ant is a type of insect, and a beetle is an insect also.

1.

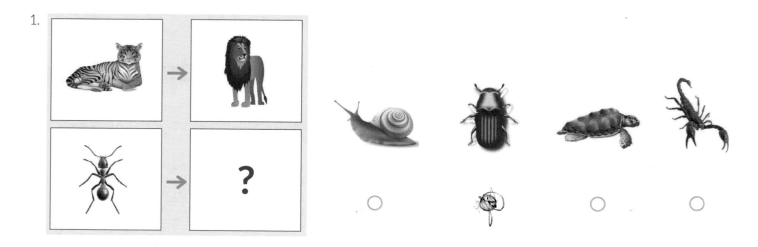

2.

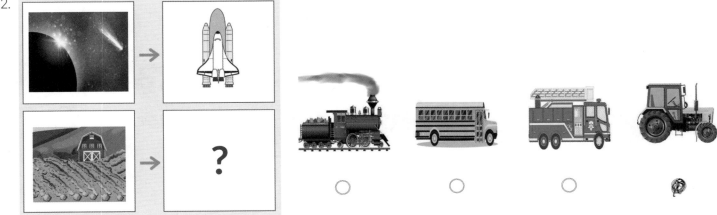

3.

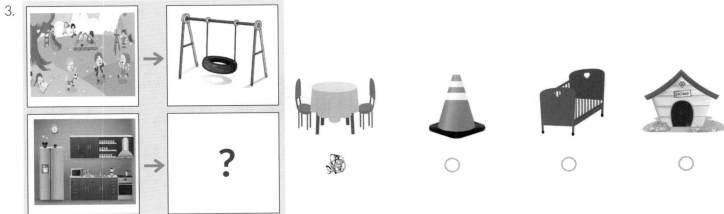

4.

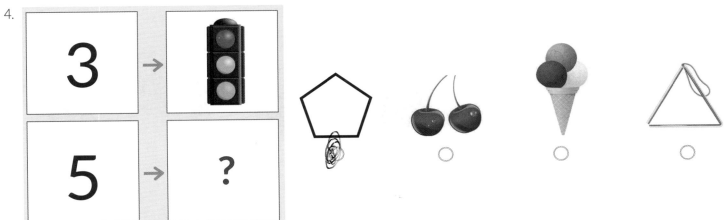

5.

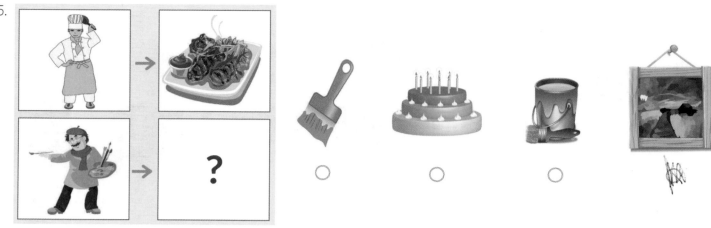

6.

7.

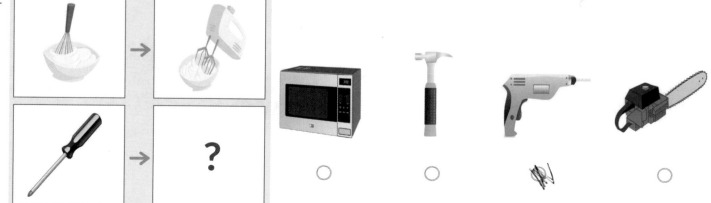

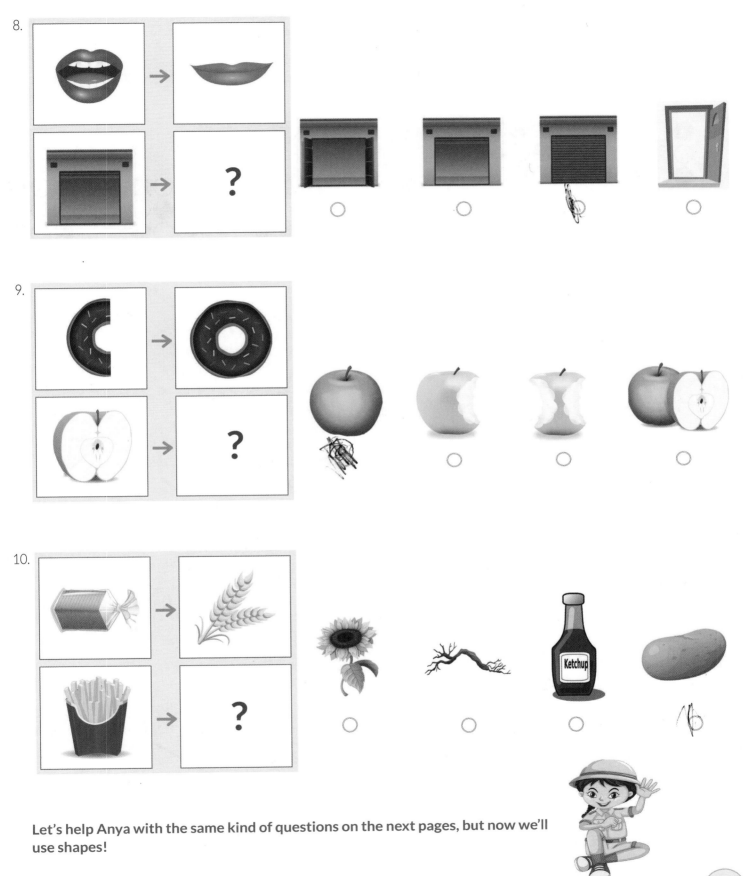

8.

9.

10.

Let's help Anya with the same kind of questions on the next pages, but now we'll use shapes!

Parent Note: As you did with Picture Analogies, together, come up with a "rule" to describe how the top set is related. With Figure Analogies, often this rule will describe how the picture in the left box "changes" into the picture in the right box.

1.

2.

3.

4.

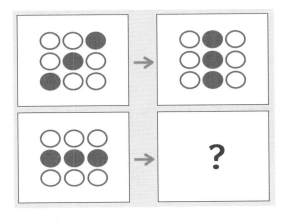

5.

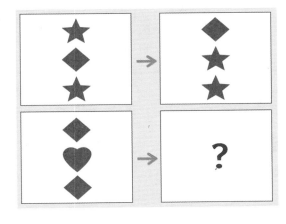

6.

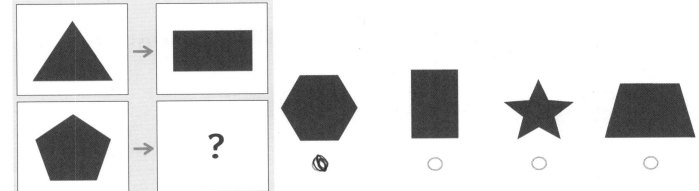

7.

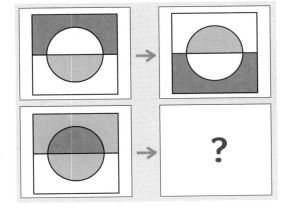

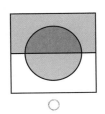 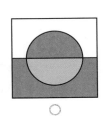 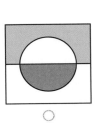 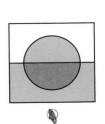

WILL YOU HELP FREDDIE FIGURE OUT THESE PUZZLES?

Directions: Look at the top row of pictures. These pictures are alike in a certain way. Then, look at the pictures that are on the bottom row. Which picture that is in the bottom row would go best with the pictures that are in the top row?

Example (read this to your child): Look at the top row of pictures. We see a police officer, a veterinarian, and a trash collector. Let's come up with a "rule" to describe how they each are alike. Look at them carefully. These are all "community helpers." They are people who help others. It is their job to help others. Look at the bottom row. Let's find the answer that follows the same rule. We see a robot, a fairy, a wizard, and a firefighter. Which one goes best with the pictures in the top row? The firefighter. The firefighter helps others.

Parent note: When your child finds answer choices that do not follow the "rule," (s)he should eliminate them. If (s)he finds more than one choice following the rule, then (s)he should come up with a more specific rule.

3.

U   O   E

W

○   ○

4.

○   ○   ○

5.

○   ○   ○

6.

7	9	15

3		F	26
	○	○	○

7.

         (remote)

○   ○   ○

8.

○   ○   ○

9.

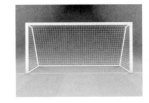  

10.

11.

Freddie needs more help - this time using shapes.
Which picture on the bottom row goes best with the pictures in the top row?

1.

2.

3.

4.

5.

6.

7.

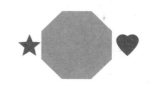  

   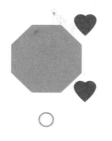

○   ○   ○   ○

8.

      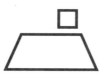

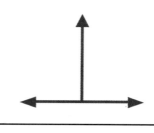         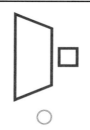

○   ○   ○   ○

9.

      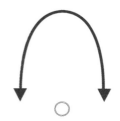   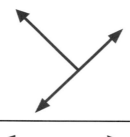 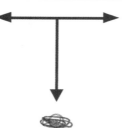

○   ○   ○   ○

10.

11.

12.

LET'S HELP SOPHIE ANSWER THESE QUESTIONS.

Directions: Listen to the question and then choose your answer.

Parent Note: These exercises are similar to those on the Sentence Completion section of the COGAT®. Try to read each question only one time to your child so that (s)he can practice listening skills.

1. If you wanted to see a reflection, which one of these objects would you use?

○   ○   ○

2. In which one of these locations would a weather forecaster predict a blizzard?

○   ○   ○

3. If your family wanted to make a budget, which of these objects would be the most helpful?

○   ○   ○   ○

4. Which one of these pictures shows something modern?

5. If you were an astronomer, which of these would you most likely use at work?

6. Your friend, Sophie, is a cellist. Which one of these instruments would she play?

7. Which one of these things would an electrician not repair?

8. Which animal does not experience metamorphosis?

9. If you were lost, which one of these would help you find your destination?

10. Your friend, Alex, is traveling in the desert. Which one of these would he be using to travel?

11. Which of these foods is produced by an animal?

MILK

12. The fruits Max used to make a fruit salad were watermelon, grapes, blueberries, strawberries, and apples. Which fruit did Max not use to make his fruit salad?

○   ○   ○   ○

13. Which choice shows a car beneath a square and a ball above a triangle?

   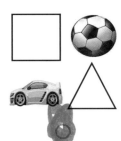   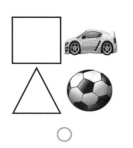   

○   ○   ○   ○

14. Which picture shows a boy with glasses, playing with a ball next to a bike?

○   ○   ○   ○

15. To complete an art project, Sophie used different art supplies. Some of these supplies are in the following pictures. She used glue, paper, colored pencils, and scissors. Which kind of supply did she not use?

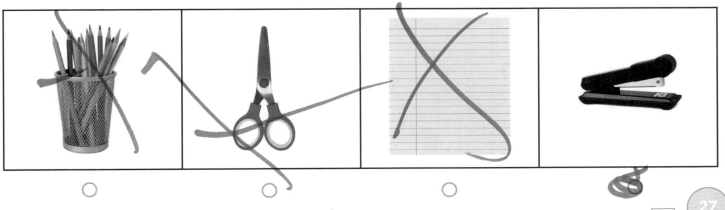

○   ○   ○   ○

LET'S GIVE ALEX A HAND!

Directions: The top row of pictures show a sheet of paper, how it was folded, and how holes were made in it. Look at these pictures on the bottom row. Which picture shows how the paper would look after the paper is unfolded?

Important Notes: Make sure your child pays attention to:
- the number of shapes and the size of the shapes
- the direction the shapes are pointing
- how the paper is folded, i.e., <u>how many times</u> and in which direction
(for some questions the paper is folded more than once)

To help your child better understand these exercises, you may wish to demonstrate using real paper and a hole puncher (or scissors).

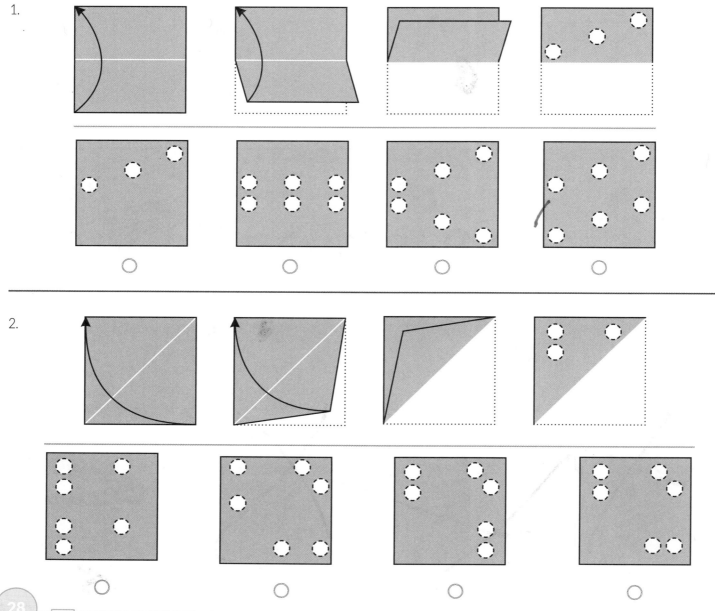

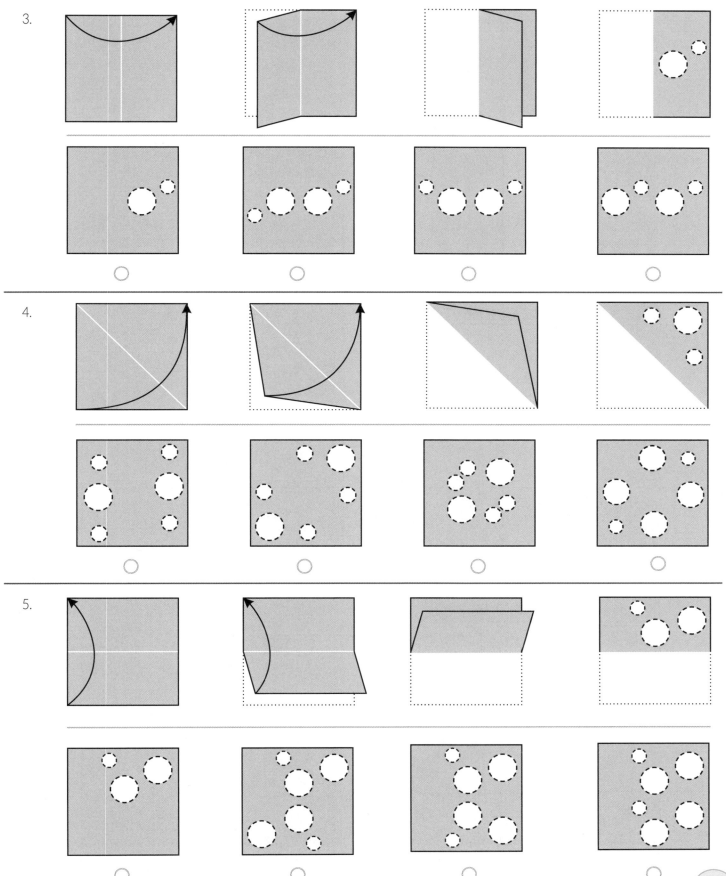

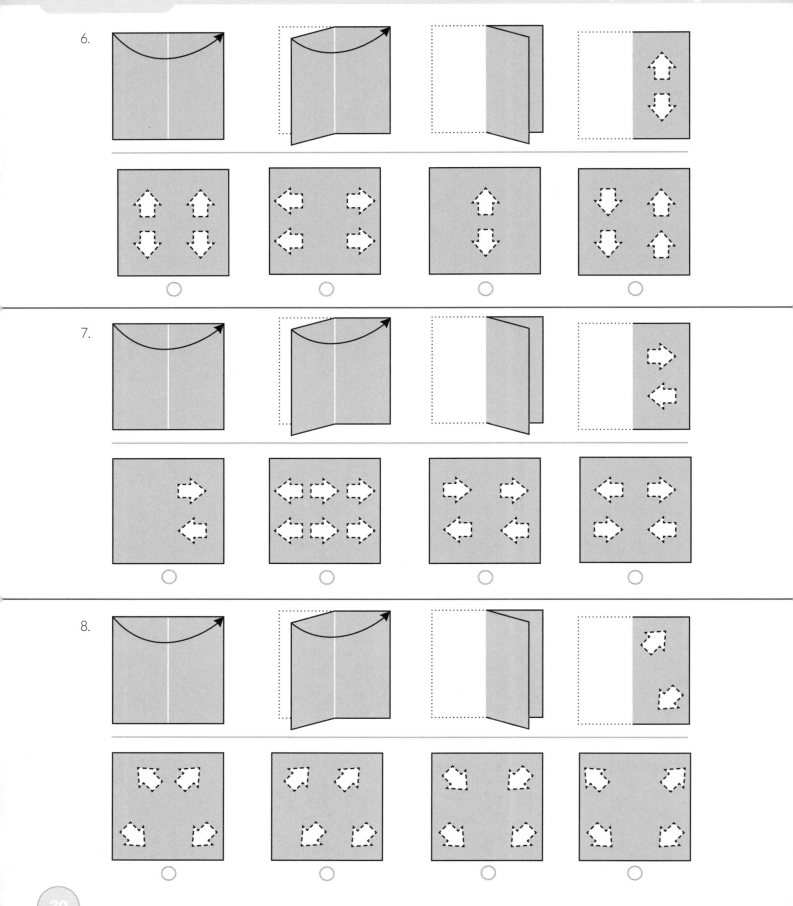

LET'S HELP ALEX WITH A FEW OTHERS!

Directions: The top row of pictures show a sheet of paper, how it was folded, and how holes were made in it. Look at these pictures on the bottom row. Which picture shows how the paper would look after the paper is unfolded?

(Here, the scissors simply show that the paper was cut.)

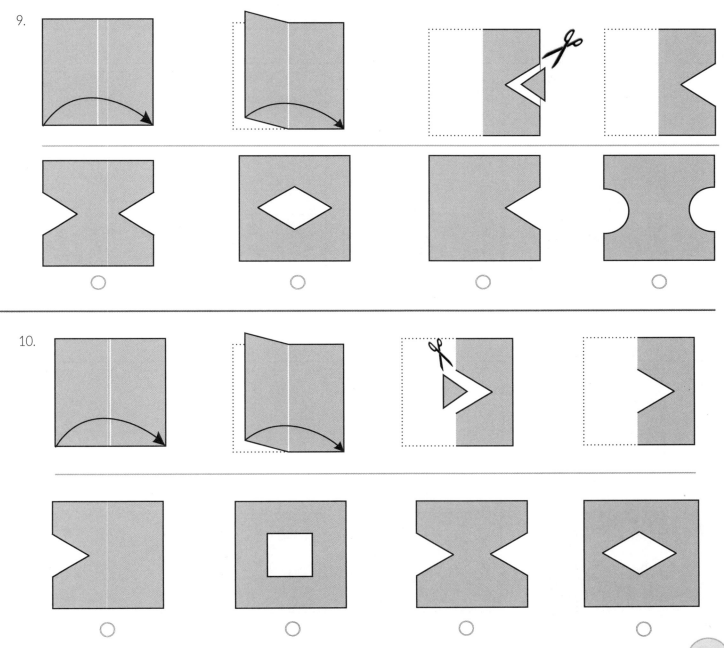

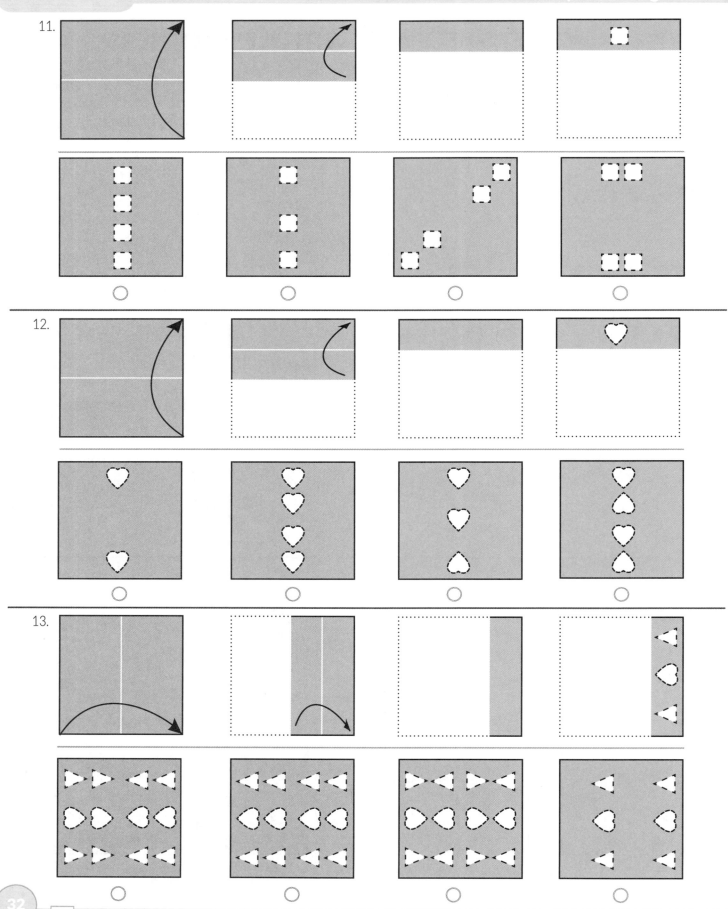

14.

15.

16.

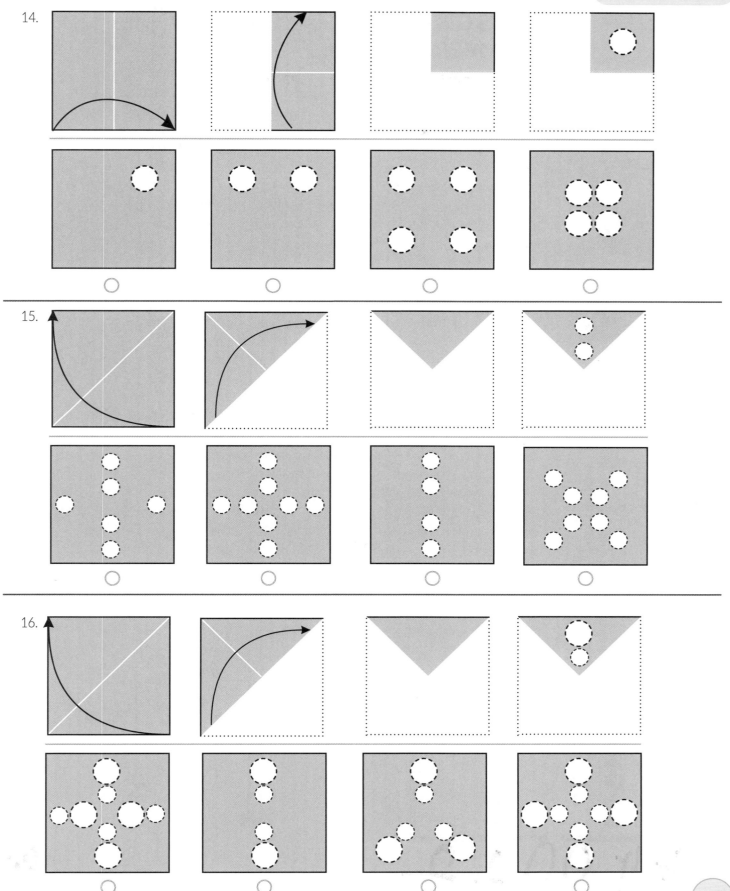

LET'S GIVE MAY A HAND WITH SOME NUMBER PUZZLES.

I NEED YOUR HELP!

Section explanation: In this section, the final rod of the abacus is missing. Before the missing rod, the rods of the abacus have a pattern. Have your child look closely at these to determine the pattern. (S)he will then need to select which rod would finish the pattern. Make sure your child carefully and correctly counts the number of abacus beads. Note that some answer choices do not have any beads. This equals "0". The gray line on some rods is to facilitate counting. (Here, the questions with bead counts greater than five have these after the fifth bead.) Due to the complexity of this question type, we have included detailed directions for the first question.

Directions for first question: Here's an abacus. The "circles" on the abacus are beads. These beads are on rods. The beads in the first five rods have made a pattern. Look at the last rod on the abacus. The beads on this rod are missing.

Next to the abacus are four rods. These are the answer choices. Choose which rod would go in the place of the last rod in order to complete the pattern.

Let's look at the abacus. We see 4 beads, then 4 beads, then 0 beads, then 0 beads, then 2 beads. Do you see a pattern? There are 2 rods with 4 beads each, followed by 2 rods with 0 beads each. There is a pair of rods with the same number of beads (4), followed by a different pair of rods with the same number of beads (0). What would go after the rod with 2 beads? The last rod on the abacus is missing. What rod goes here to finish the pattern? (Look at each answer choice.) It is the rod with 2 beads.

Directions for the rest: Which rod would go in the place of the missing rod to finish the pattern?

1.

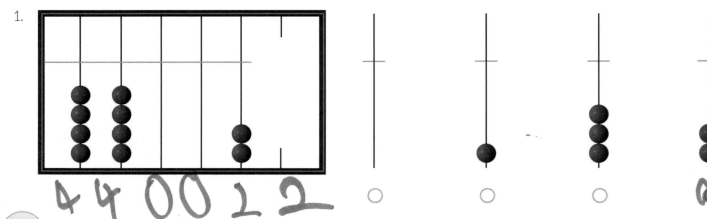

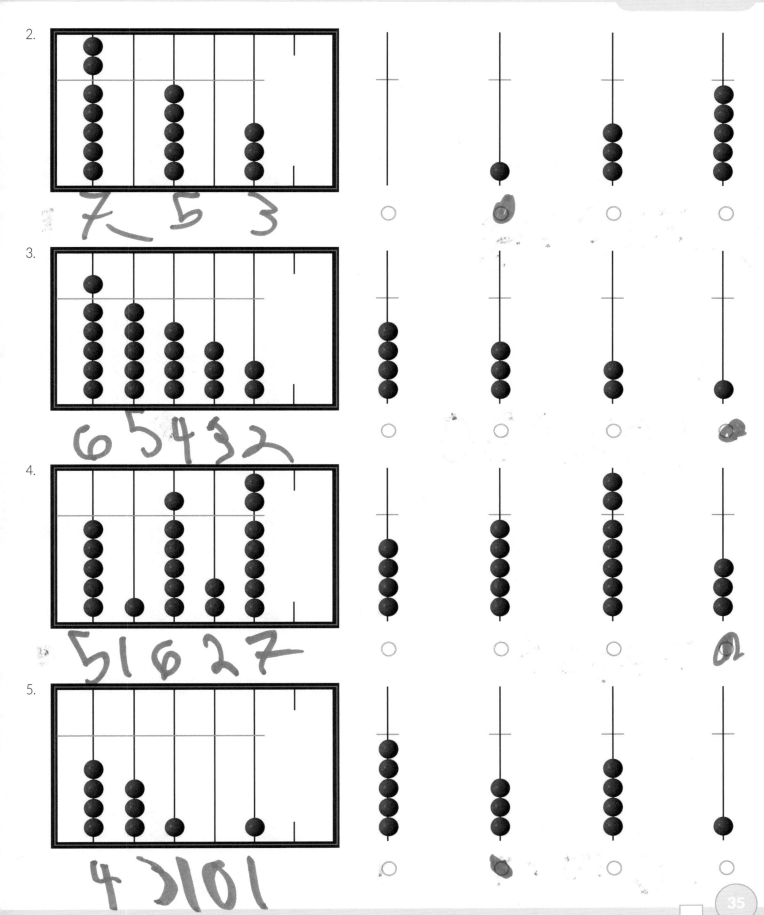

2. 7 5 3

3. 6 5 4 3 2

4. 5 6 2 7

5. 4 3 0 1

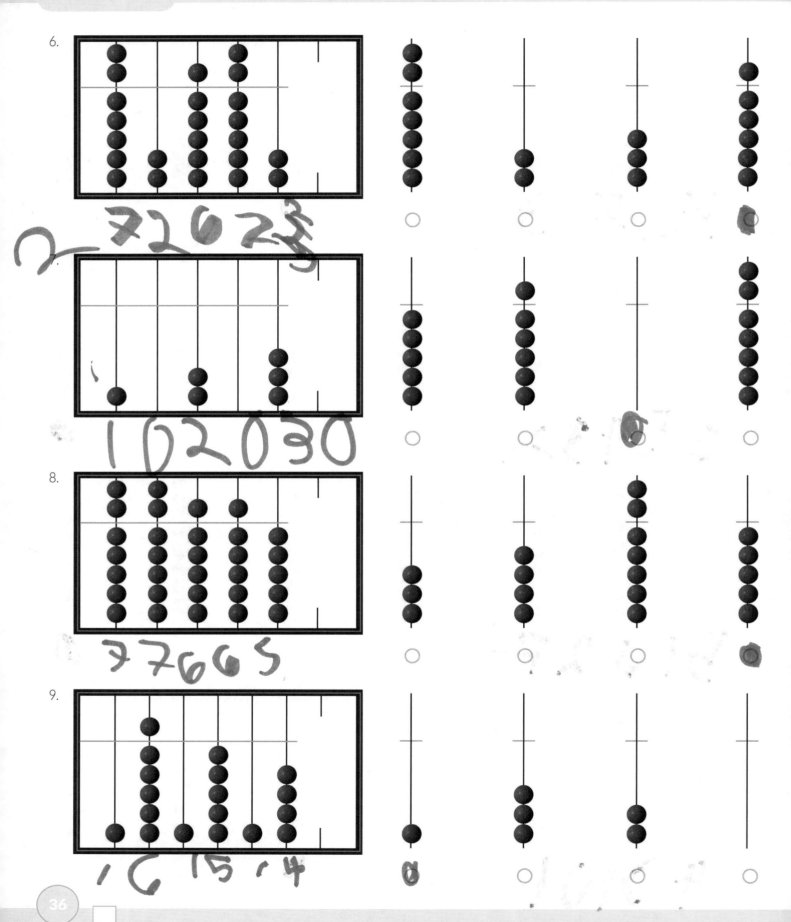

6.

7. 3 72623

10 20 30

8. 77665

9. 16 15 14

LET'S DO SOME MORE!

MAY NEEDS YOUR HELP WITH MORE NUMBER GAMES!

Directions: Look at the box that has the question mark. Which number would go here so that both of the sides of this equal sign (point to the equal sign) would have the same amount?

Parent Note: Some exercises require three numbers to be added/subtracted. In these, be sure your child correctly distinguishes between the addition and subtraction signs and completes the entire exercise before selecting an answer.

1.

| 6 | = | 5 | + | ? |

0   1   2   3

2.

| 4 | = | 9 | - | ? |

3   4   5   6

3.

3 + 5

| 8 | = | 2 | + | 1 | + | ? |

5   3   7   8

4.

9 - 2

| 7 | = | 8 | + | 1 | - | ? |

0   1   2   3

5.

9 - 6 = 3

| 3 | = | 10 | - | 1 | - | ? |

4   5   6   7

= 5

6.

3 +

| 5 | = | 11 | - | 8 | + | ? |

2   3   4   5

= 2

7.

4 + 0

| 4 | = | 12 | - | 8 | + | ? |

4   2   1   0

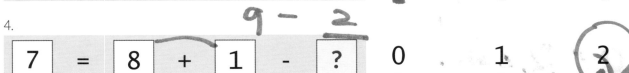

8. $9 = 12 + 4 - ?$ 3 4 5 7

9. $7 = 0 + 9 - ?$ 2 3 4 6

10. $5 = 15 + 2 - ?$ 12 9 5 8

11. $0 = 13 - 5 - ?$ 9 8 0 18

12. $8 = 4 + 12 - ?$ 6 7 8 9

13. $4 = 9 - 3 - ?$ 0 1 2 3

14. $15 = 9 + 2 + ?$ 5 4 3 1

15. $14 = 14 - 0 - ?$ 1 2 3 0

16. $7 = 10 - 8 + ?$ 0 4 5 3

17. $0 = 9 + 4 - ?$ 13 0 9 4

18. $9 = 15 - 8 + ?$ 0 2 4 8

19. $0 = 1 + 4 - ?$ 0 9 5 4

20. $2 = 13 - 4 - ?$ 15 4 8 7

21. $3 = 11 + 1 - ?$ 0 9 8 7

22. $2 = 6 + 4 - ?$ 0 2 8 7

23. $2 = 7 + 3 - ?$ 8 2 0 9

24. $11 = 12 - 1 - ?$ 1 2 3 0

25. $4 = 10 - 3 - ?$ 4 3 2 1

26.
$3 = 18 - 18 + ?$ 1 2 3 4

27.
$2 = 13 - 9 - ?$ 0 1 3 2

28.
$8 = 19 - 8 - ?$ 3 2 0 4

29.
$5 = 15 - 5 - ?$ 5 10 1 0

30.
$9 = 17 - 9 + ?$ 2 1 8 9

31.
$19 = 4 + 3 + ?$ 18 5 12 4

32.
$18 = 9 + 3 + ?$ 12 5 6 4

33.
$3 = 19 - 4 - ?$ 1 12 3 10

34.
$4 = 11 - 8 + ?$ 3 2 1 0

35.
$12 = 11 + 8 - ?$ 3 7 2 6

36.
$3 = 10 - 8 + ?$ 3 2 1 0

37.
$2 = 18 - 9 - ?$ 7 1 6 9

38.
$14 = 1 + 2 + ?$ 10 7 8 11

39.
$4 = 14 - 4 - ?$ 9 6 7 14

40.
$9 = 13 - 12 + ?$ 7 8 9 0

41.
$3 = 19 - 4 - ?$ 1 12 3 15

42.
$7 = 17 - 4 - ?$ 6 7 5 13

43.
$17 = 19 - 11 + ?$ 0 7 9 8

MAY NEEDS A HAND WITH NUMBER GAMES!

Section explanation: Number analogies questions are similar to the other analogies earlier in this book. Here, however, the top set of boxes and the bottom set of boxes must have the same type of quantitative relationship. Your child must figure out which one of the answer choices would go in the empty box with the question mark to complete the mathematical analogy. Due to the complexity of this section, we have included detailed directions for the first question.

Directions for first question: The top boxes belong together in some way. Look at the top box on the left - there are 9 cones. Look at the top box on the right - there are 6 cones. What has changed between the picture on the left and the picture on the right? We need to come up with a "rule" to describe what has happened. The right box has 3 less cones than the left box. Three cones were taken away to get the number of cones in the right box.

Next, let's look carefully at the boxes in the bottom row. The first box has 5 hats. The second box is empty. Look carefully at the row of pictures next to the boxes. Which one of these goes in the empty box? The answer is "2 hats." This is 3 hats less than the left box. In the row, the last choice has 2 hats.

Directions for the rest: Which answer choice would go inside the empty box at the bottom?

1.

2.

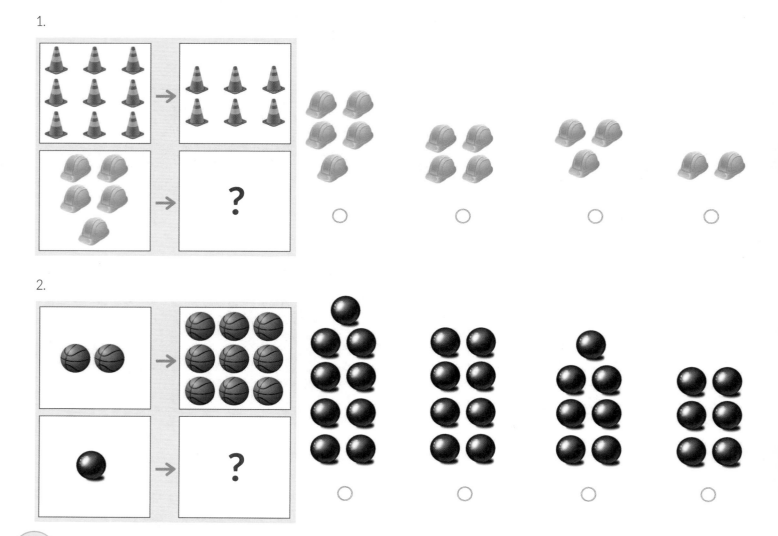

3.

4.

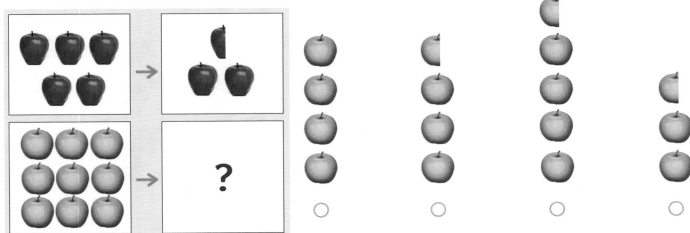

5.

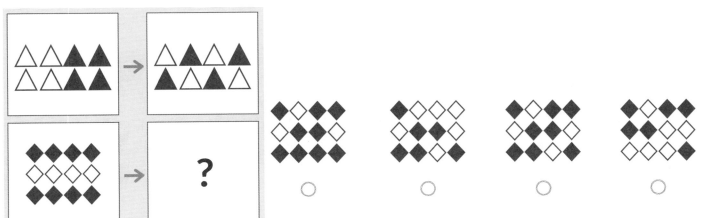

6.

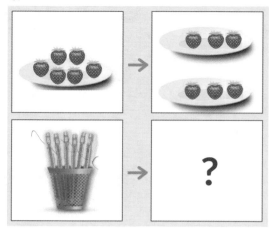

○

○

○

7.

○ ○ ○

8.

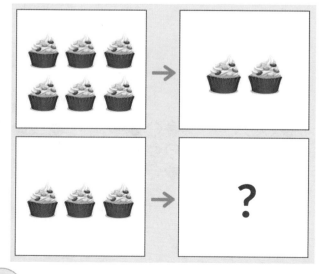

○ ○ ○

9.

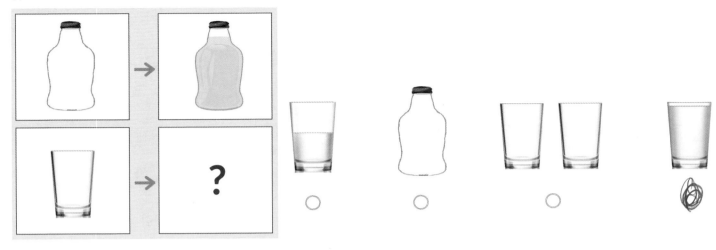

10.

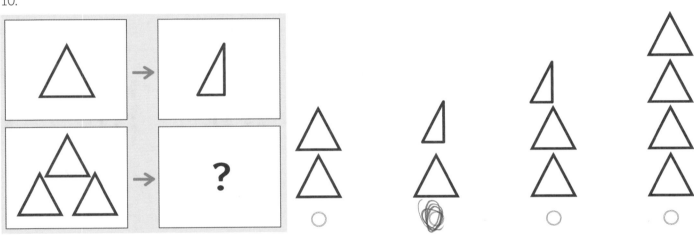

11.

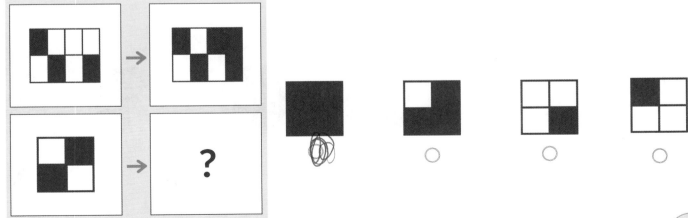

12.

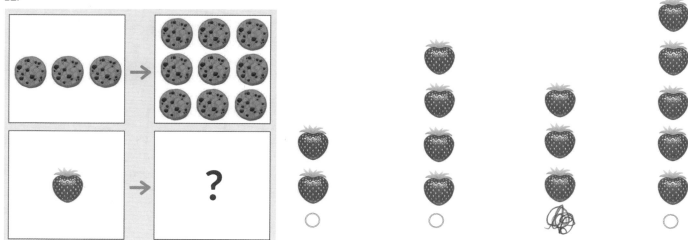

13.

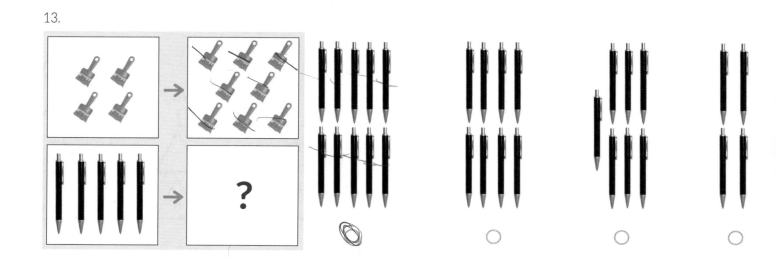

14.

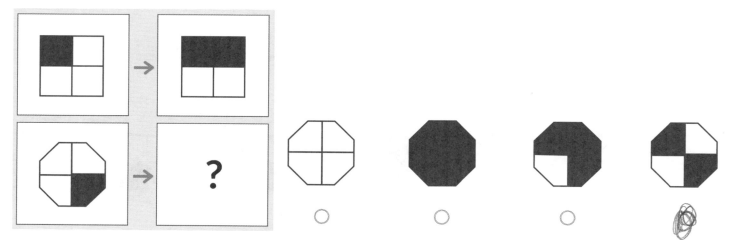

PRACTICE QUESTION SET INSTRUCTIONS

✂ Please cut out pages 89-93. Pages 89-93 are the Directions and Answer Key for the Practice Question Set. They include question prompts.

Reading Directions: Tell your child to listen carefully (like a detective!), because you can read the directions to him/her only one time. (Test administrators often read directions only once.)

Test instructors will not let your child know if his/her answers are correct/incorrect. If you wish for the Practice Question Set to serve as a "practice test," then as your child completes the Practice Question Set, we suggest you do the same. Instead of saying if answers are correct/incorrect, you could say "Nice work, let's try some more."

Navigation Figures: Assuming your child has completed the Workbook, then (s)he is familiar with the exercise format (navigating through pages with rows of questions). To make the test navigation easier for kids, some gifted tests use image markers in place of question numbers and in place of page numbers.

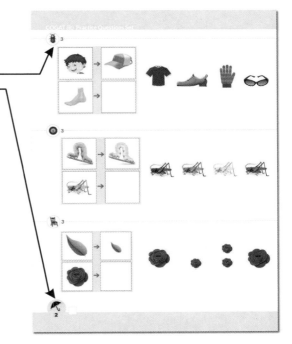

We include the "markers" so that your child can be familiar with them.

When your child needs to look at a new page, you would say, for example, "Find the page where there is an umbrella at the bottom." When your child needs to look at a question, you would say, for example, "Find the row where there is a bug."

These markers are listed on the Directions & Answer Key pages so that you can read them to your child.

The Practice Question Set is divided into three sections, to mirror the different "batteries" of the COGAT®: Verbal Section (pages 46-59), the Quantitative Section (pages 60-73), and the Non-Verbal Section (pages 74-87).

Time: Allow one minute per question, approximately.

Evaluation: The Practice Question Set is labeled by question type. After your child is done, on your own (without your child) go through the Set by question type, writing the number answered correctly in the space provided on the answer key. While these practice questions are not meant to be used in place of an official assessment, these will provide a general overview of strengths/weaknesses, as they pertain to test question type. For questions your child didn't answer correctly, go over the question and answer choices again with him/her. Compare the answer choices, specifically what makes the correct answer choice the right choice. Since gifted programs typically accept only top performers, we encourage additional practice.

We offer another COGAT® Grade 2 book as well as free questions in e-book format.
See page 94 for details.

1.

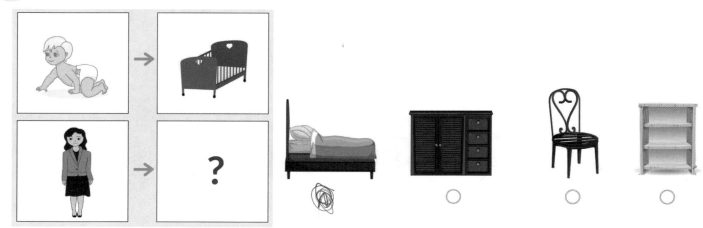

 2.

one pedle

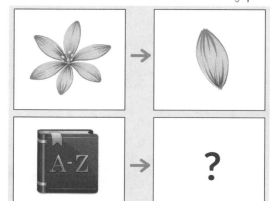

one page

  3.

4.

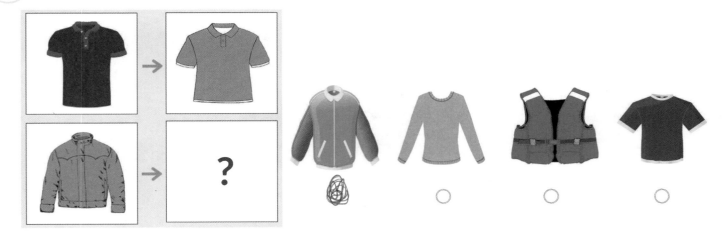

5.

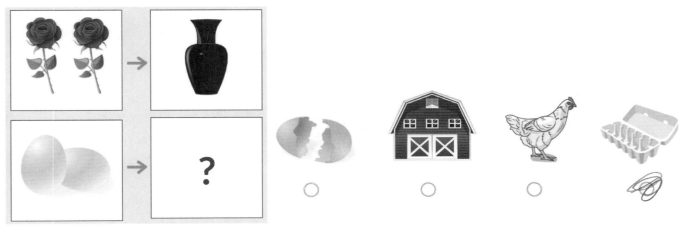

6.

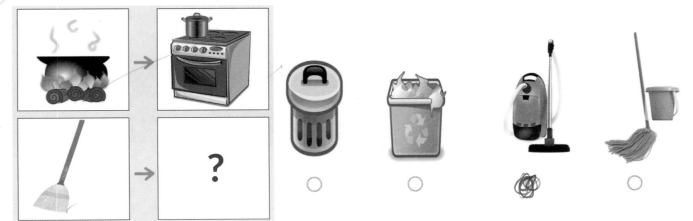

7.

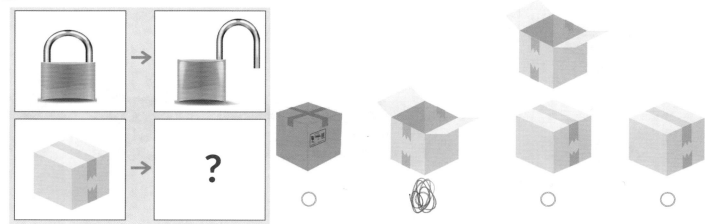

 8.

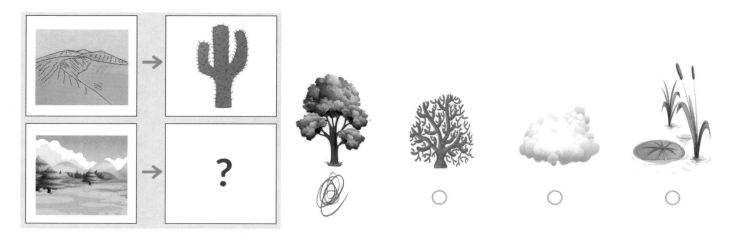

 9.

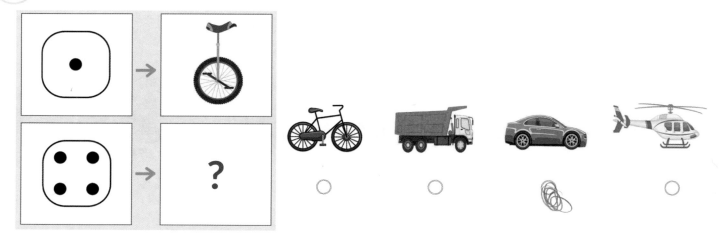

10.

11.

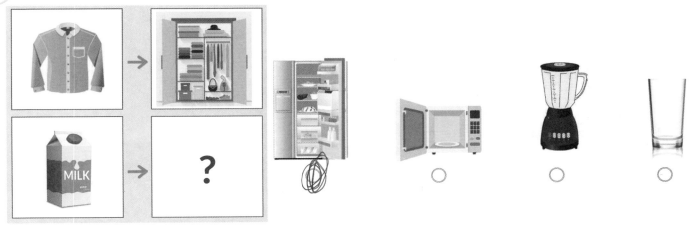

12.

13.

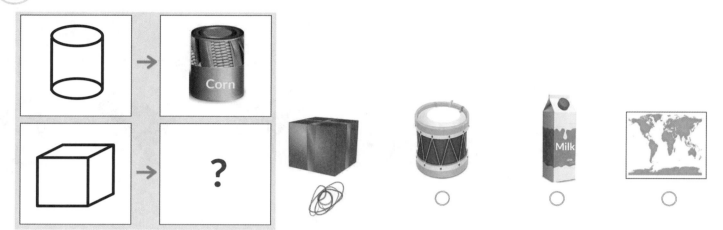

 **14.**

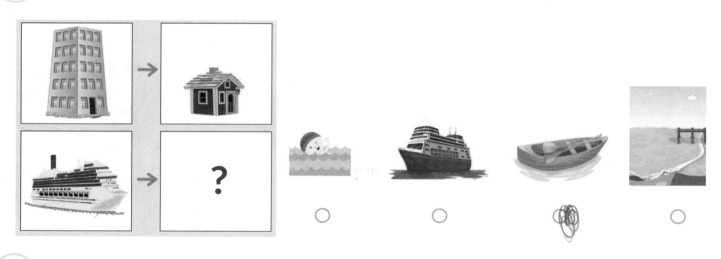

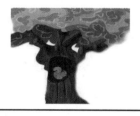 **15.**

16.

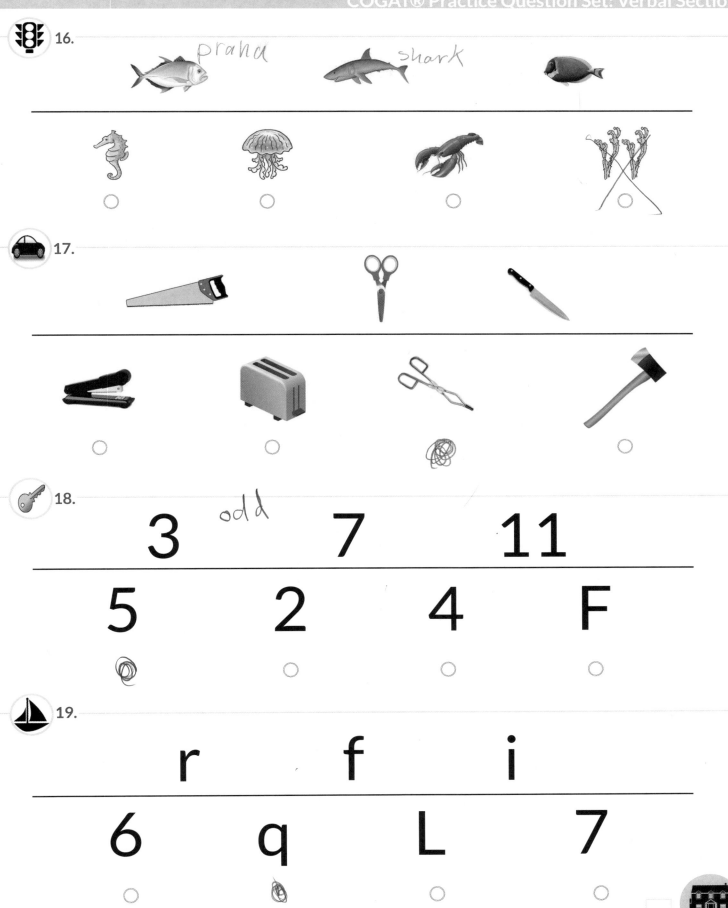

praha   shark

17.

18.

odd

3   7   11

5   2   4   F

19.

r   f   i

6   q   L   7

20.

21.

22.

L X W

5 h U S

23.

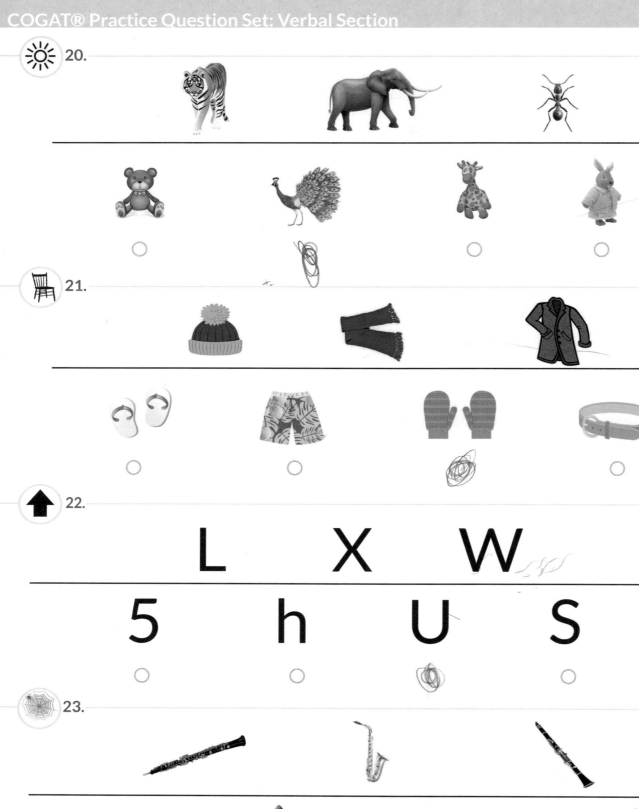

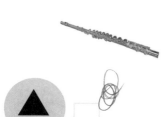

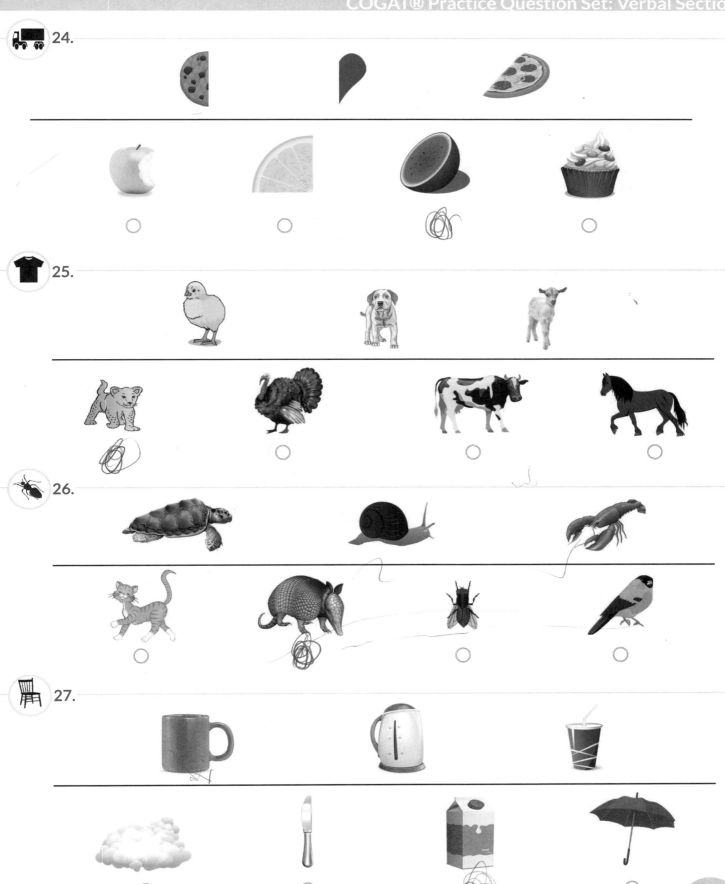

24.

25.

26.

27.

28.

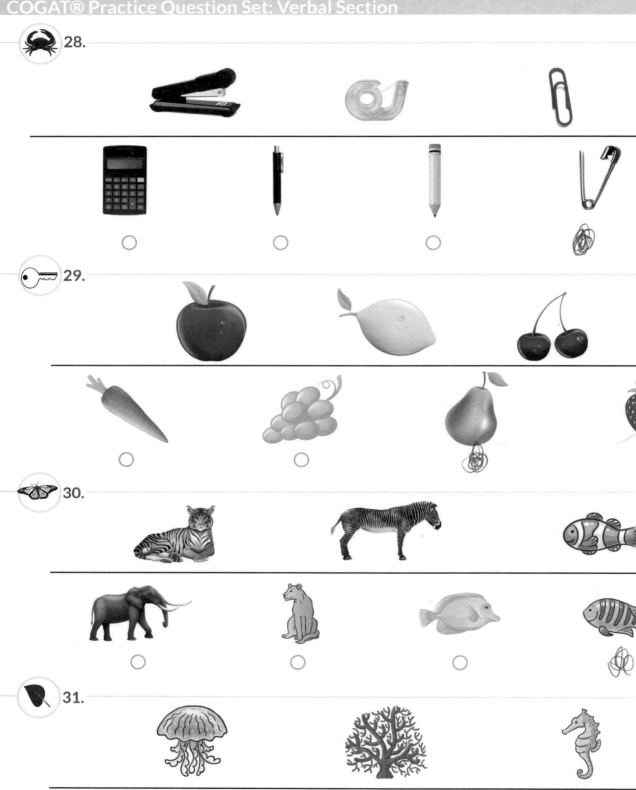

29.

30.

31.

32.

○　　　○　　　○　　　○

 33.

  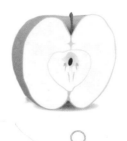 

○　　　○　　　○　　　○

 34.

○　　　○　　　○　　　○

 35.

 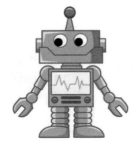  

○　　　○　　　○　　　○

 36.

○   ○   ○   ○

 37.

○   ○   ○   ○

 38.

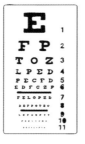  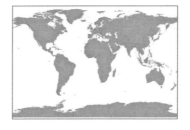 

○   ○   ○   ○

 39.

○   ○   ○   ○

40.

 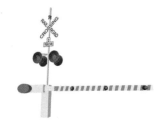  

○ ○ ○ ○

 41.

○ ○ ○ ○

 42.

○ ○ ○ ○

 43.

○ ○ ○ ○

★ 44.

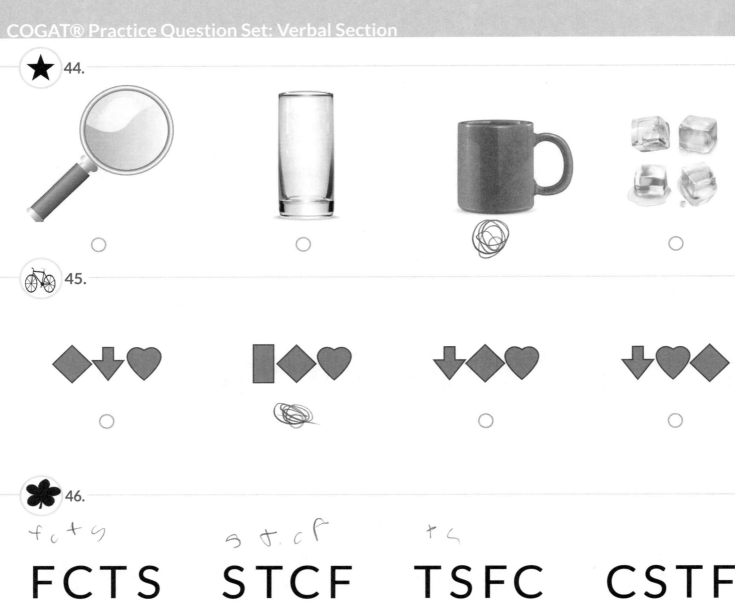

○   ○   ○   ○

45.

○   ○   ○   ○

46.

FCTS   STCF   TSFC   CSTF

○   ○   ○   ○

47.

○   ○   ○   ○

48.

 49.

 50.

51.

52.

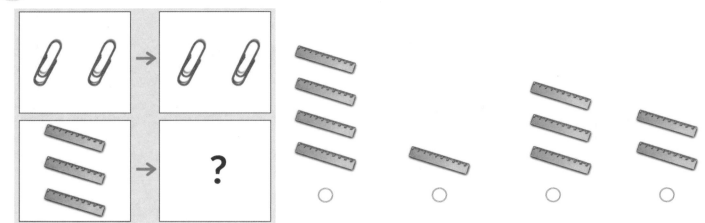

 53.

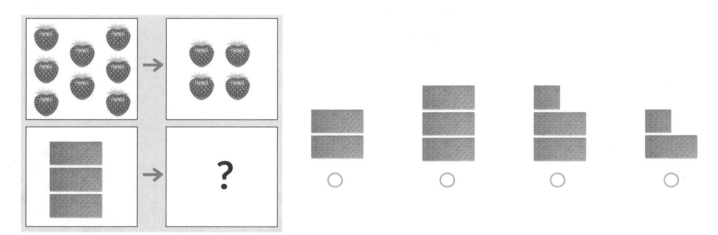

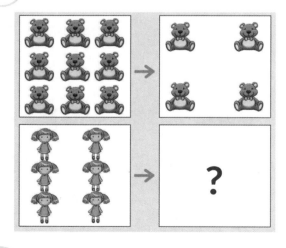 **54.**

55.

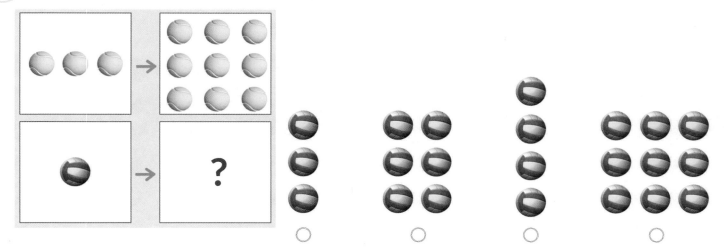

○   ○   ○   ○

 56.

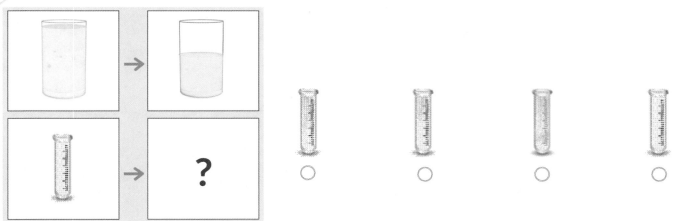

○   ○   ○   ○

 57.

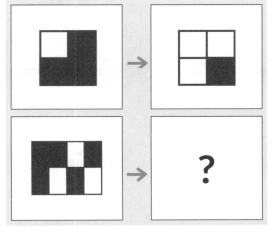

○   ○   ○   ○

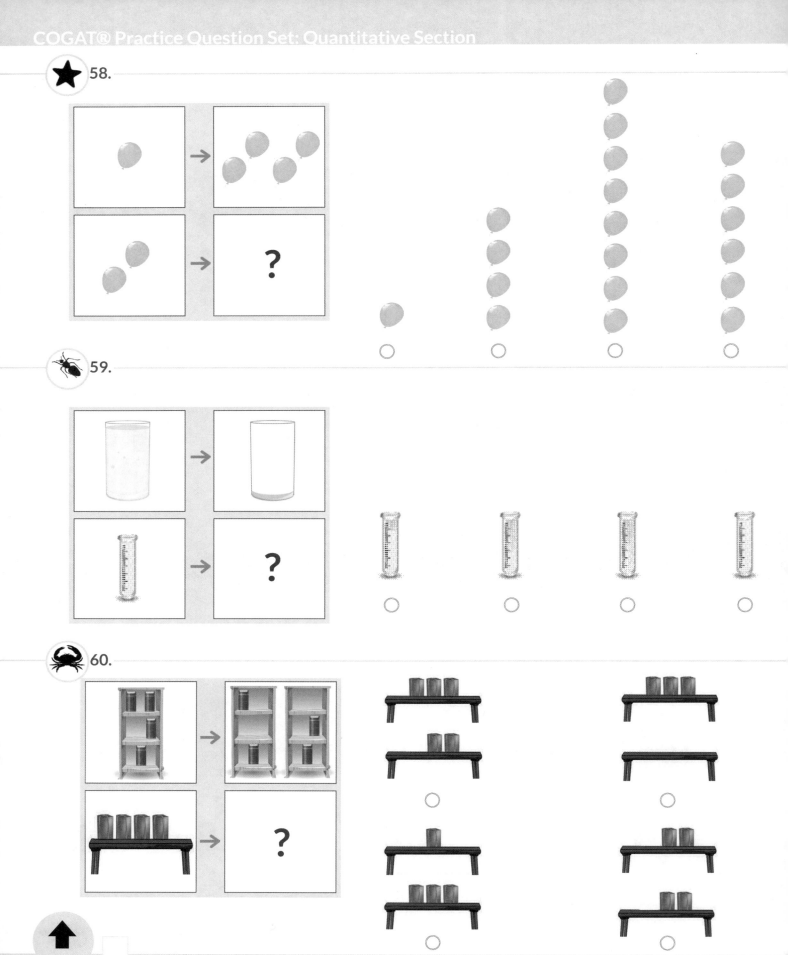

61.

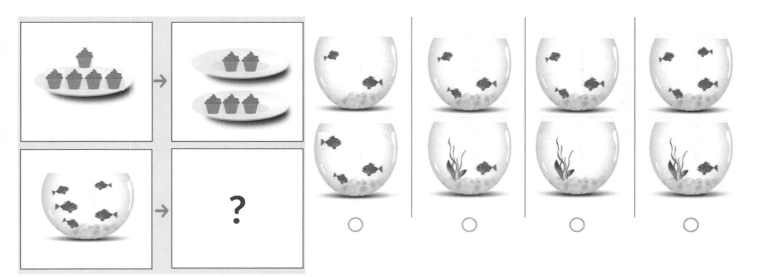

 62.

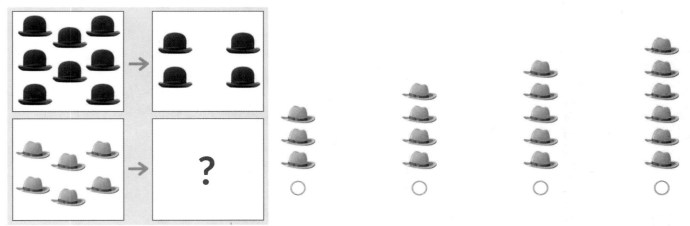

63.

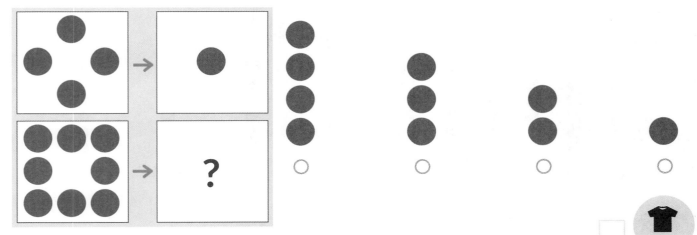

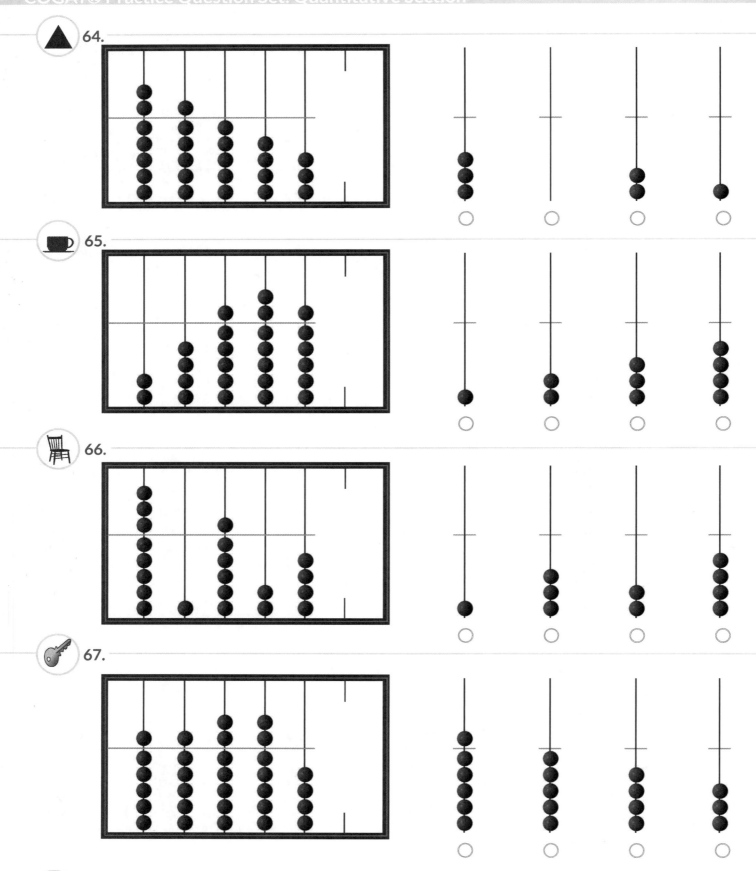

68.

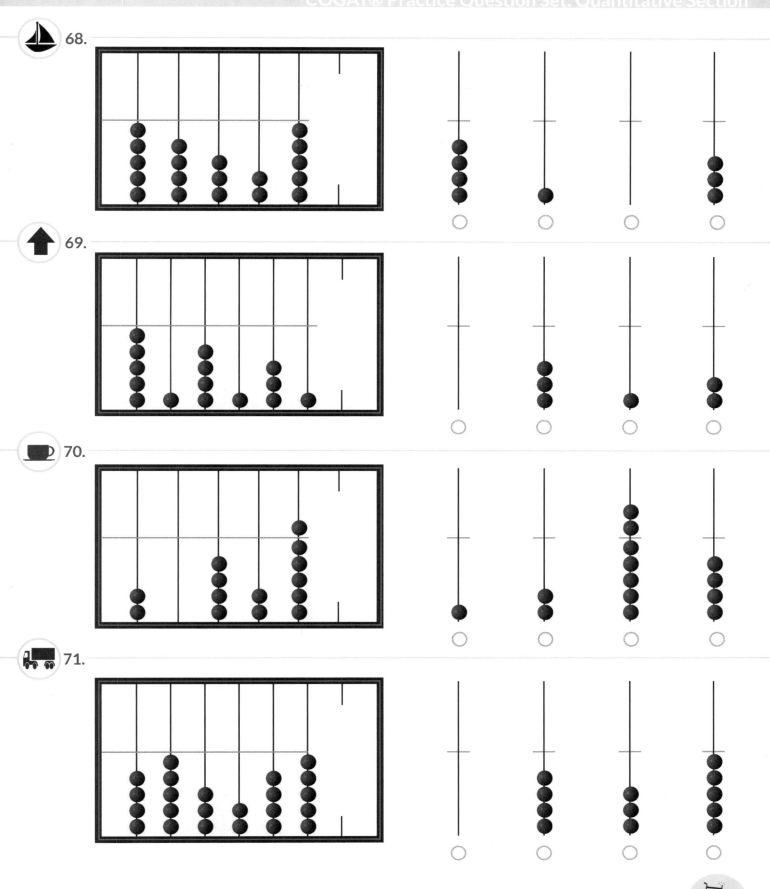

69.

70.

71.

72.

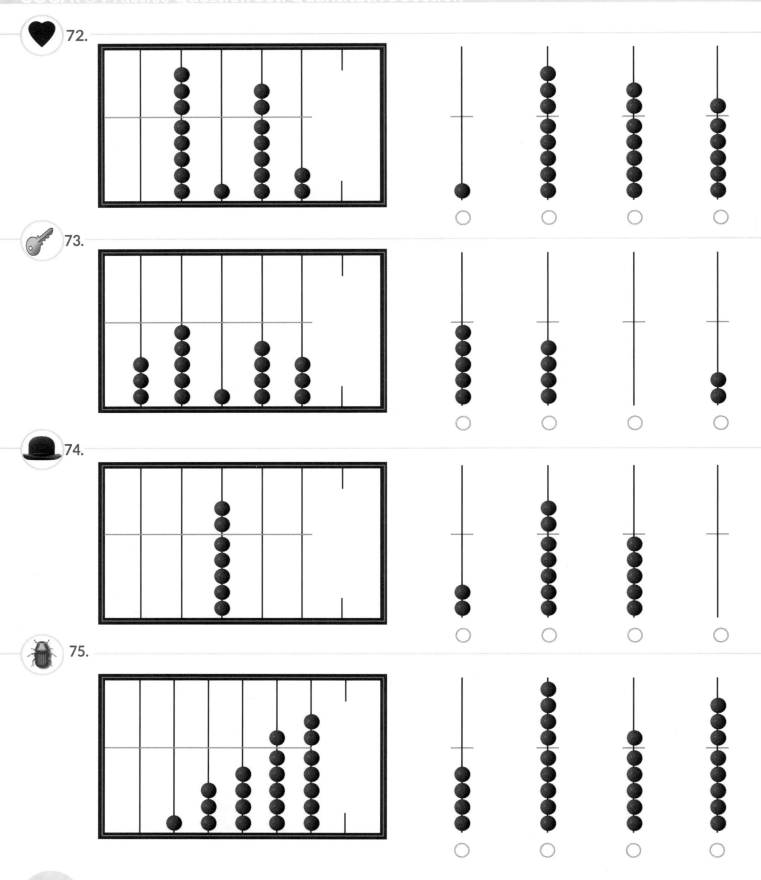

73.

74.

75.

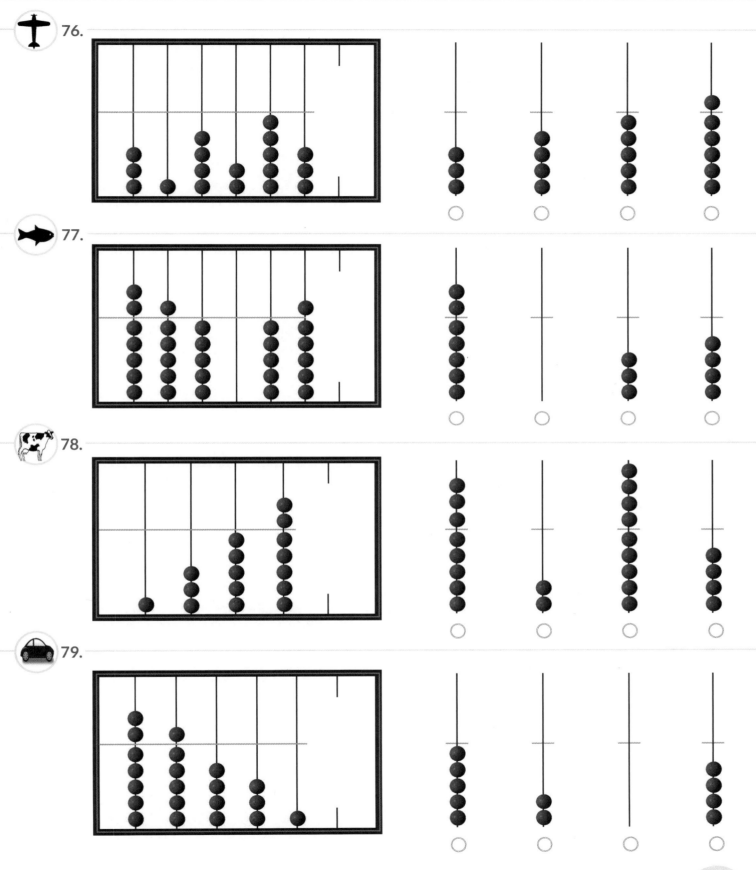

80.

7 = 2 + ?   3 ○   4 ○   5 ○   6 ○

★ 81.

8 = 6 + ?   0 ○   1 ○   2 ○   3 ○

82.

5 = 2 + 4 - ?   1 ○   2 ○   3 ○   4 ○

83.

6 = 10 - 1 - ?   0 ○   1 ○   2 ○   3 ○

84.

7 = 11 - 8 + ?   1 ○   2 ○   3 ○   4 ○

85.

4 = 9 - 8 + ?   3 ○   2 ○   1 ○   0 ○

86.

7 = 0 + ?   6 ○   7 ○   8 ○   9 ○

87.

12 = 13 - ?   1 ○   2 ○   3 ○   4 ○

88.

12 = 1 + 2 + ?   7 ○   8 ○   9 ○   10 ○

89.

1 = 10 - 1 - ?   8 ○   7 ○   6 ○   5 ○

90.

3 = 8 - 8 + ?   1 ○   2 ○   3 ○   4 ○

91.

7 = 10 - 3 + ?   3 ○   2 ○   1 ○   0 ○

 92.

0 = 10 - 1 - ?   9 ○   8 ○   7 ○   6 ○

93.

12 = 11 - 2 + ?   1 ○   2 ○   3 ○   4 ○

94.

3 = 9 - 7 + **?**   0 ○   1 ○   2 ○   3 ○

95.

5 = 12 + 2 - **?**   9 ○   5 ○   8 ○   7 ○

96.

5 = 9 + 6 - **?**   3 ○   12 ○   11 ○   10 ○

97.

6 = 15 - 1 - **?**   5 ○   10 ○   8 ○   7 ○

98.

7 = 10 - 9 + **?**   11 ○   12 ○   6 ○   5 ○

99.

14 = 9 - 8 + **?**   13 ○   12 ○   11 ○   3 ○

100.

15 = 9 + **?**   6   7   8   5

101.

$\boxed{1}$ = $\boxed{12}$ + $\boxed{3}$ - $\boxed{?}$ 15 ○   14 ○   8 ○   16 ○

★ 102.

$\boxed{9}$ = $\boxed{11}$ - $\boxed{1}$ - $\boxed{?}$ 3 ○   4 ○   5 ○   1 ○

103.

$\boxed{13}$ = $\boxed{7}$ + $\boxed{1}$ + $\boxed{?}$ 7 ○   4 ○   5 ○   6 ○

104.

$\boxed{12}$ = $\boxed{0}$ + $\boxed{12}$ - $\boxed{?}$ 3 ○   2 ○   12 ○   0 ○

105.

$\boxed{7}$ = $\boxed{13}$ + $\boxed{1}$ - $\boxed{?}$ 7 ○   5 ○   8 ○   6 ○

106.

$\boxed{0}$ = $\boxed{15}$ - $\boxed{15}$ + $\boxed{?}$ 15 ○   0 ○   10 ○   11 ○

107.

| 2 | = | 9 | + | 5 | - | ? | 12 ○ | 2 ○ | 11 ○ | 10 ○ |

108.

| 0 | = | 10 | - | 5 | - | ? | 0 ○ | 10 ○ | 5 ○ | 15 ○ |

109.

| 13 | = | 7 | + | 4 | + | ? | 10 ○ | 1 ○ | 9 ○ | 2 ○ |

110.

| 9 | = | 9 | + | 2 | - | ? | 3 ○ | 2 ○ | 1 ○ | 0 ○ |

111.

| 14 | = | 11 | + | 5 | - | ? | 8 ○ | 10 ○ | 12 ○ | 2 ○ |

112.

| 10 | = | 7 | - | 3 | + | ? | 5 ○ | 0 ○ | 6 ○ | 11 ○ |

113.

| 1 | = | 16 | + | 3 | - | ? | 12 ○ | 8 ○ | 19 ○ | 18 ○ |

★ 114.

| 8 | = | 19 | - | 2 | - | ? | 3 ○ | 4 ○ | 9 ○ | 8 ○ |

115.

| 18 | = | 12 | + | 3 | + | ? | 5 ○ | 9 ○ | 4 ○ | 3 ○ |

116.

| 17 | = | 13 | + | 6 | - | ? | 13 ○ | 19 ○ | 10 ○ | 2 ○ |

117.

| 1 | = | 11 | + | 8 | - | ? | 2 ○ | 18 ○ | 7 ○ | 17 ○ |

118.

| 10 | = | 19 | - | 17 | + | ? | 3 ○ | 2 ○ | 4 ○ | 8 ○ |

119.

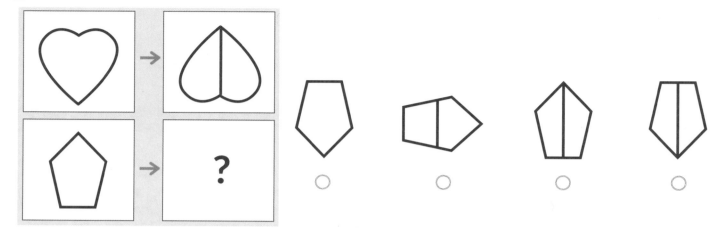

120.

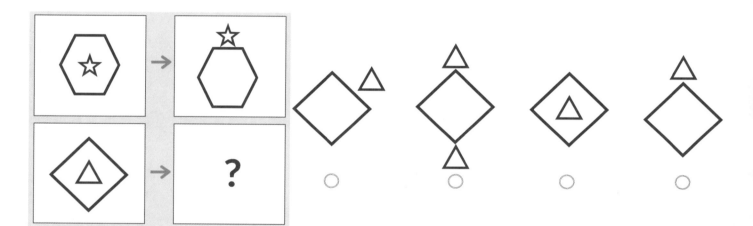

121.

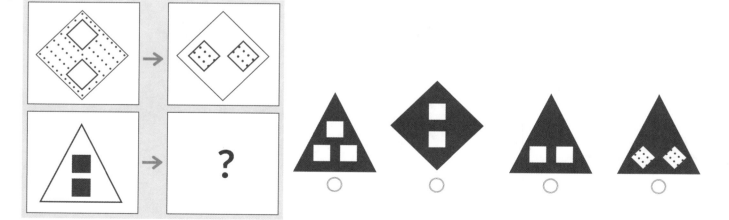

122.

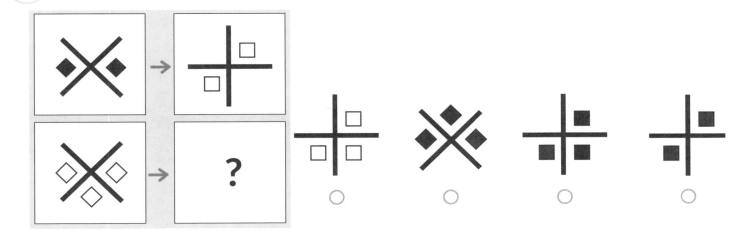

123.

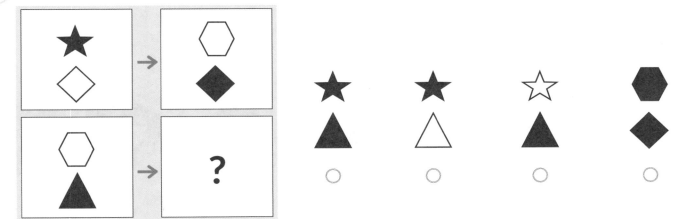

124.

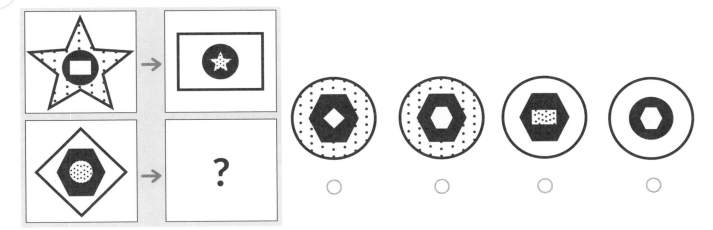

125.

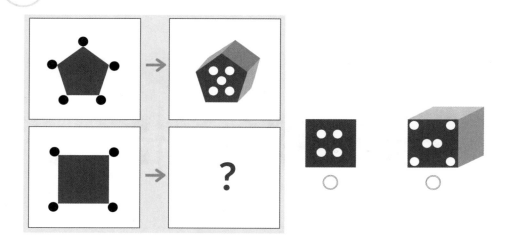

126.

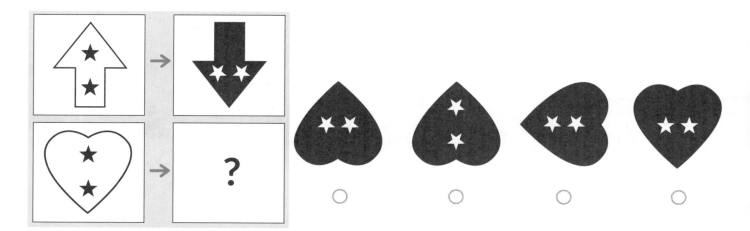

127.

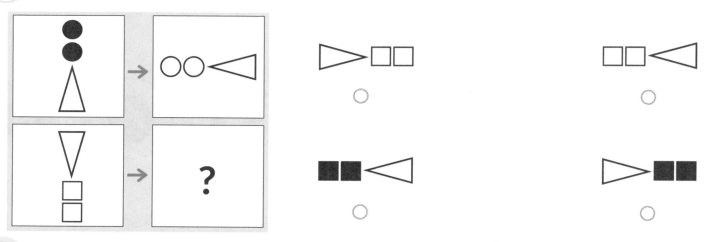

128.

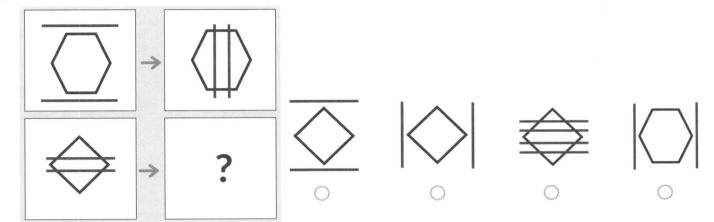

 129.

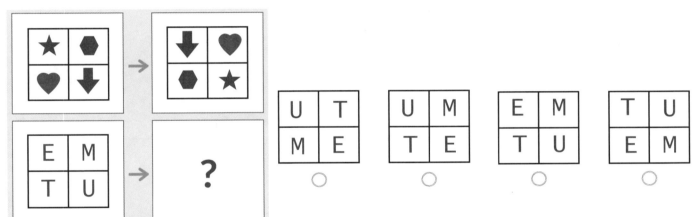

 130.

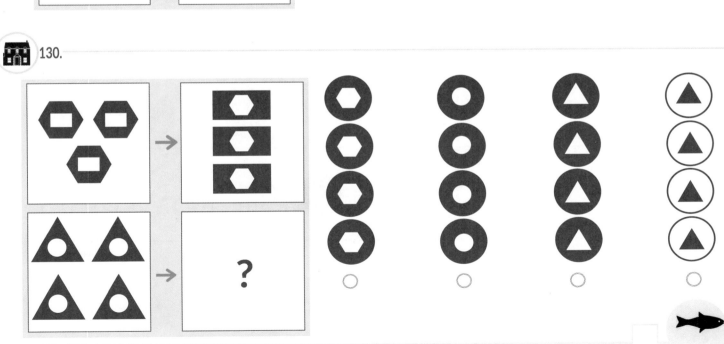

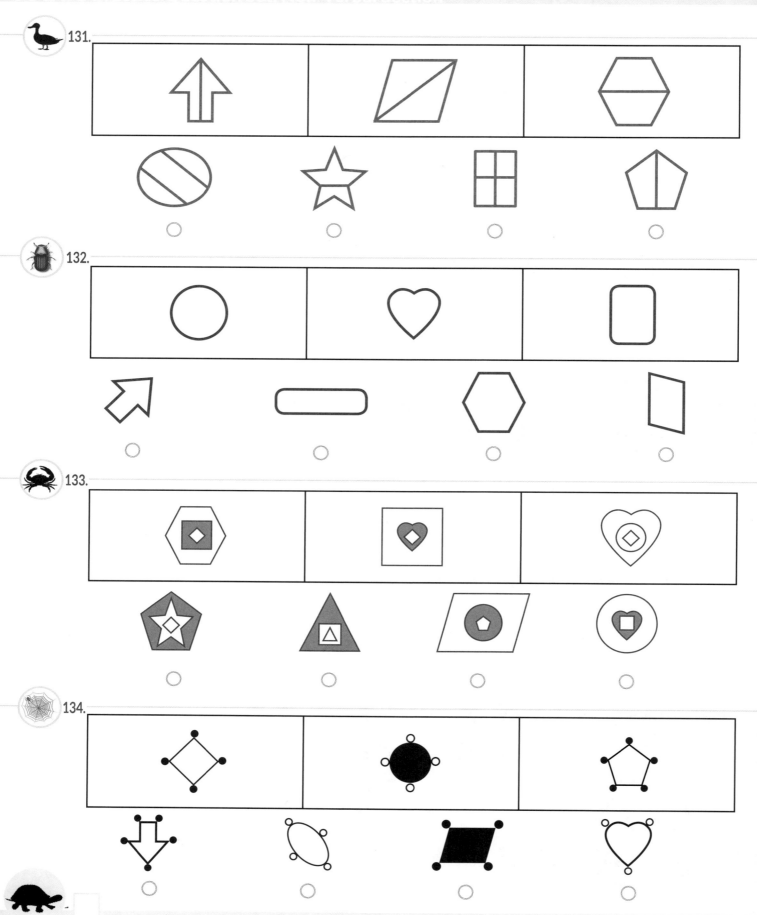

131.

132.

133.

134.

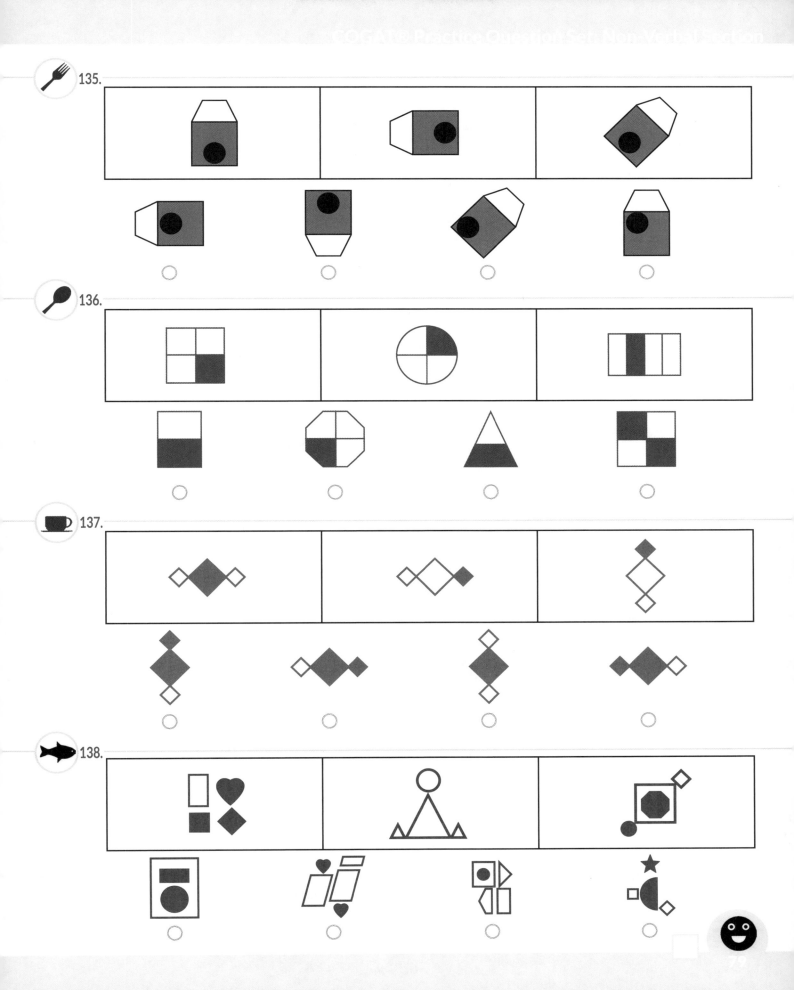

135.

136.

137.

138.

139.

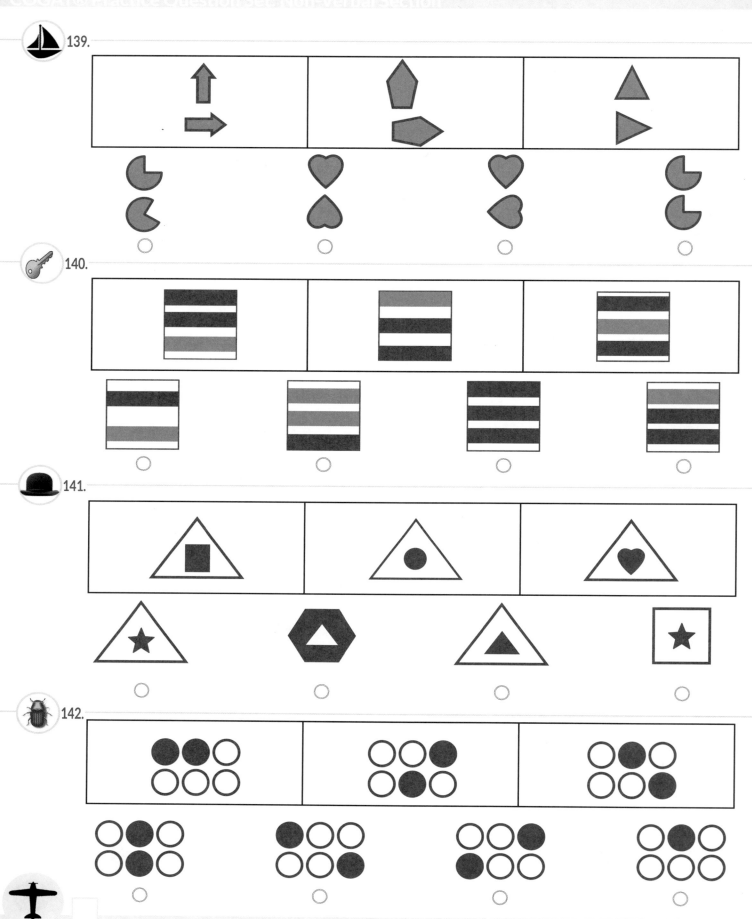

140.

141.

142.

143.

144.

145.

146.

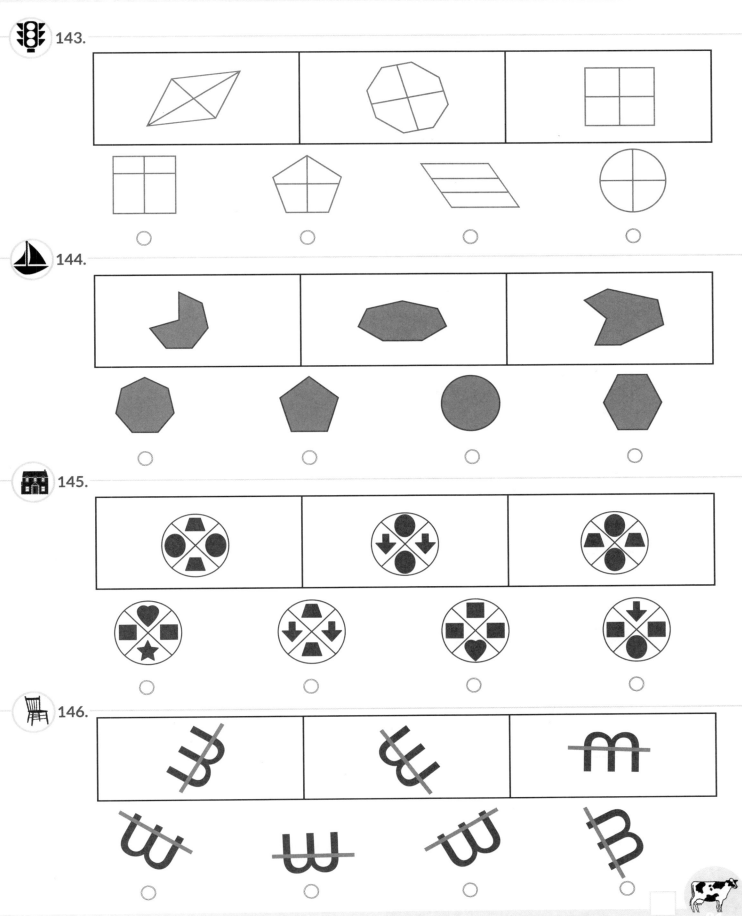

147.

148.

149.

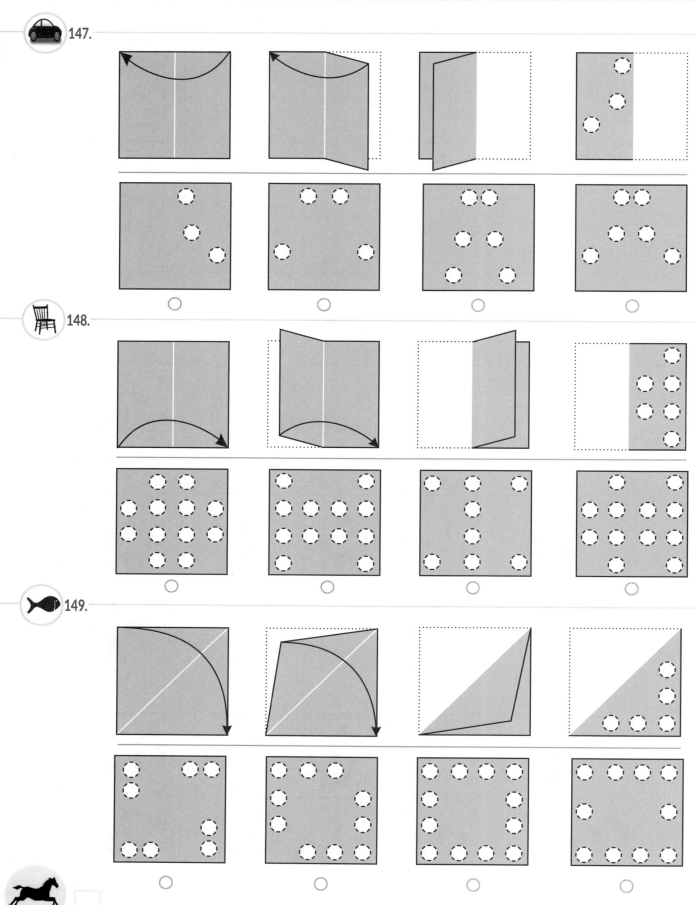

150.

151.

152.

153.

154.

155.

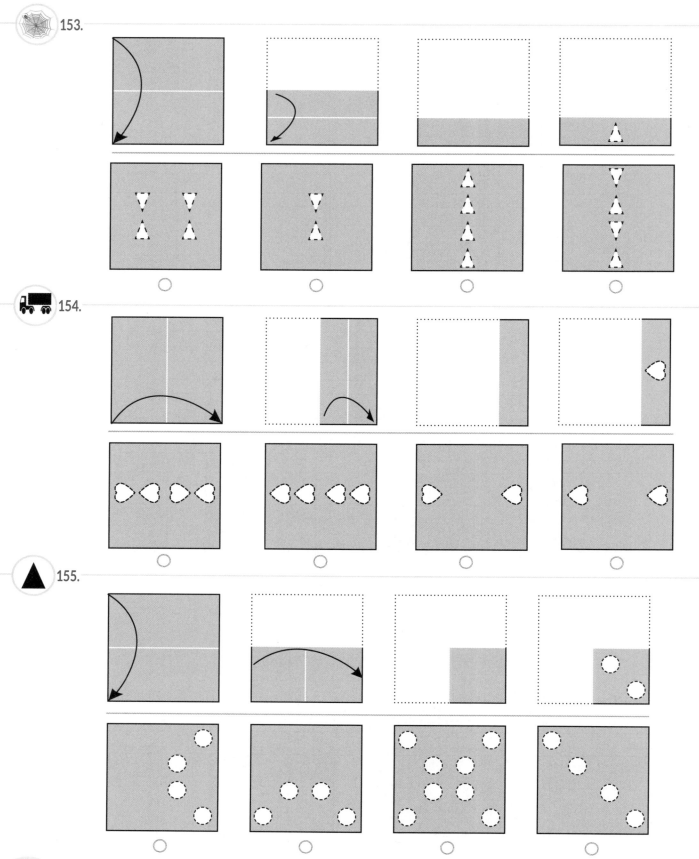

156.

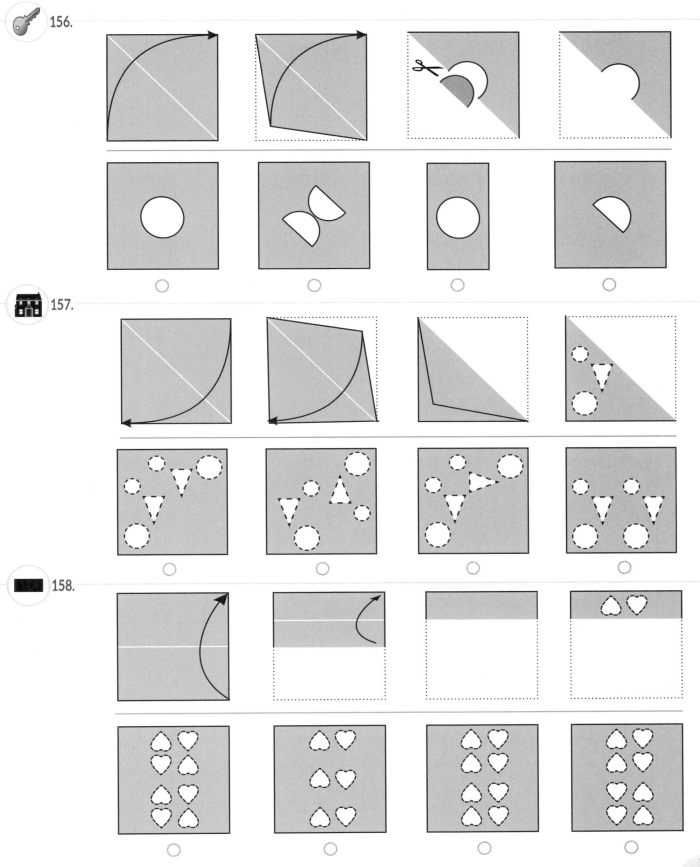

157.

158.

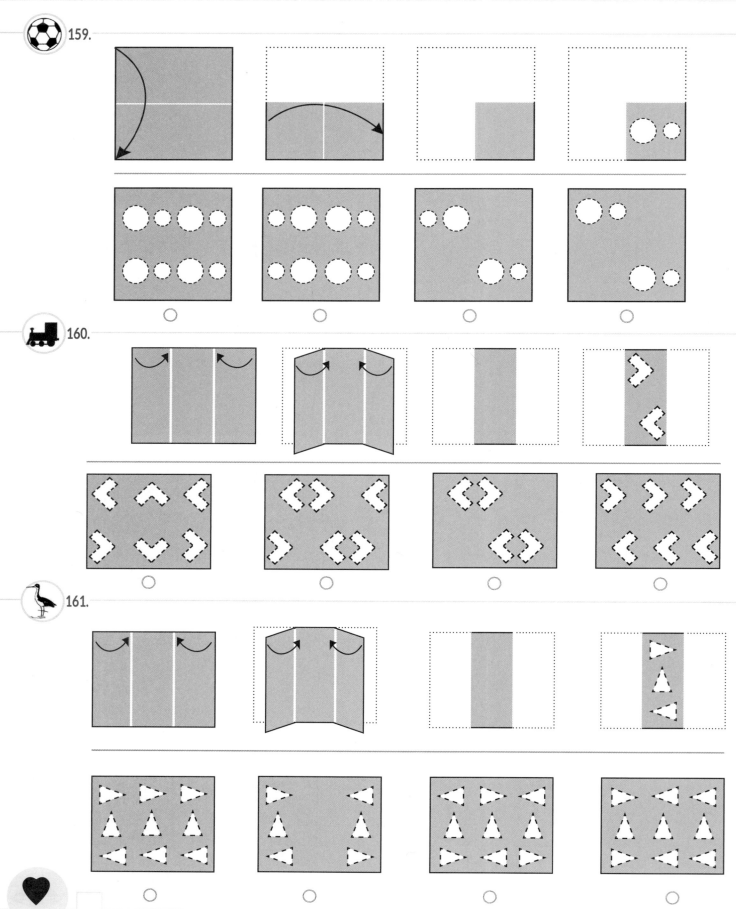

159.

160.

161.

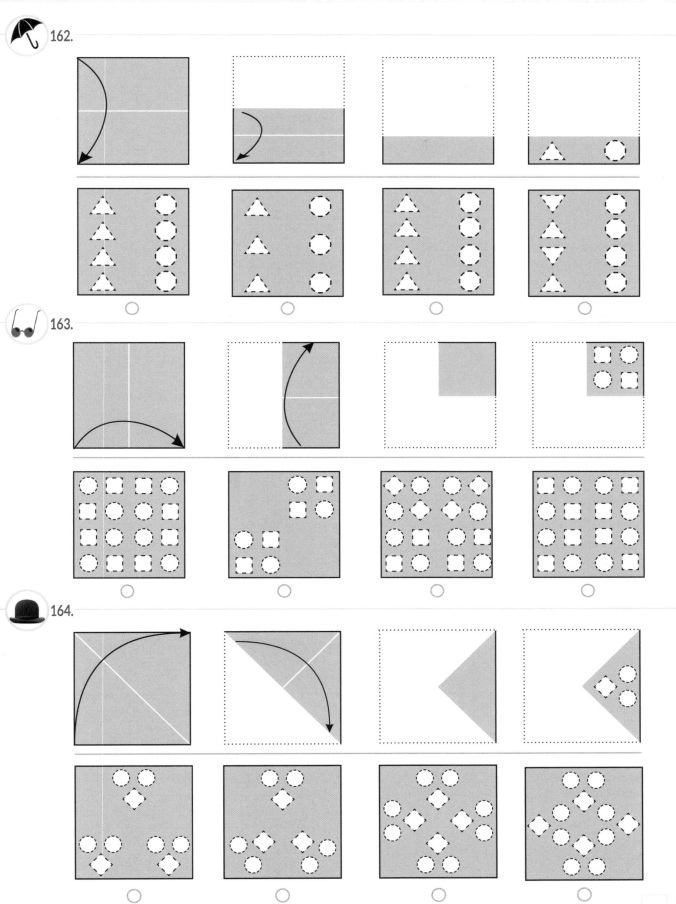

162.

163.

164.

ANSWER KEY FOR WORKBOOK (p.10-44)

Picture Analogies

1. B
2. D (vehicle > place vehicle used/place vehicle found)
3. A (location > item found in location)
4. A (a stoplight has 3 lights; a pentagon has 5 sides)
5. D (a chef creates meals; a painter creates paintings)
6. B (opposites: happy/sad; day/night)
7. C (slower action done by hand > faster version of action done with electrical item)
8. C (open > closed)
9. A (half > whole)
10. D (food > object food comes from (wheat/potato))

Figure Analogies

1. C (white circles become blue; blue become white -or- the same design is in upper left/lower right and upper right/lower left)
2. B (1 more line added inside shape)   3. D (rotates clockwise)
4. A (# of sides increases by 1; 3 sides > 4 sides; 5 sides > 6 sides)
5. B (circles line up diagonally bottom left to top right, then line up vertically; on the bottom they do the opposite: circles line up horizontally, then line up diagonally top left to bottom right)
6. C (same number & type of shapes in top boxes; same number & shape types in bottom boxes; top two shapes switch positions)
7. D (squares are divided in half & circles are also; from left to right, square halves switch color & circle halves switch color)

Picture Classification

1. D
2. B (made from types of grain)
3. C (uppercase vowels)
4. C (reptiles)
5. C (animal homes)
6. A (odd numbers)
7. C (used to measure)
8. D (toys)
9. C (sports goals)
10. B (sports balls)
11. A (hot things)

Figure Classification

1. D (lines inside circle go from lower left to upper right)
2. B (same kind of shapes align horizontally: large one in middle, two smaller on right and left)
3. D (arrows pointing same direction)
4. B (6-sided shape)
5. B (same number of shapes (3))
6. A (shape divided in half)
7. C (large octagon with 1 heart, 1 star)
8. A (square is by one of the end corners of the shorter straight side of the trapezoid)
9. D (same number of arrow points)
10. D (3 shapes filled in)
11. C (half of shape filled in)
12. C (3 upside-down hearts & 1 right-side-up heart)

Can You Find It? (Sentence Completion)

1. D (mirror)
2. A (snowy mountain)
3. B (calculator)
4. C (computer)
5. D (telescope)
6. A (cello)
7. C (binoculars)
8. A (rooster)
9. D (compass)
10. A (jeep)
11. C (milk)
12. C (bananas)
13. B
14. C
15. D (stapler)

Paper Folding Puzzles

1. C	6. A	11. A	16. D
2. D	7. D	12. D	
3. C	8. A	13. C	
4. B	9. A	14. C	
5. C	10. D	15. B	

Number Series (Abacus Activity)

1. D
2. A (rods 1,3,5 decrease by 2; rods 2,4,6 = 0)
3. D (each rod decreases by 1)
4. D (rods 1,3,5 increase by 1; rods 2,4,6 increase by 1)
5. B (4-3-1-0-1-3)
6. D (7-2-6-7-2-6)
7. C (rods 1,3,5 increase by 1; rods 2,4,6 = 0)
8. D (2 of each; 7-7-6-6-5-5)
9. A (rods 1,3,5,7 = 1; rods 2,4,6 decrease by 1)

Number Puzzles

1. B	9. A	17. A	25. B	33. B	41. B
2. C	10. A	18. B	26. C	34. C	42. A
3. A	11. B	19. C	27. D	35. B	43. C
4. C	12. C	20. D	28. A	36. C	
5. C	13. C	21. B	29. A	37. A	
6. A	14. B	22. C	30. B	38. D	
7. D	15. D	23. A	31. C	39. B	
8. D	16. C	24. D	32. C	40. B	

Number Analogies

1. D   2. B (+7)   3. A (double)   4. C (half)
5. C (same number of blue shapes -or- same number of white shapes)
6. D (same 6 objects split 3 & 3)
7. A (same 4 objects split 1 & 3)   8. D (divide by 3)
9. D (empty container > same container almost full)
10. B (half)
11. A (+2 sections filled in -or- 2 less sections white)
12. C (multiply by 3)   13. A (double)
14. D (1/4 of shape filled in > 1/2 of shape filled in -or- in the second box, +1 section of shape gets filled in/-1 section of the shape is white)

COGAT® PRACTICE QUESTION SET: DIRECTIONS & ANSWER KEY

-Be sure to read 'Practice Question Set Instructions' first (page 45).
-This answer key is divided into charts according to COGAT® question type so that you can easily see how your child performs on each of the test's nine question types. Each chart includes the directions you will read to your child. It also lists the page navigation icons and question navigation icons that you will read to your child to assist with navigation.
1) If turning to a new page, say to your child: "Find the page where there is a(n) ___ at the bottom." (These sentences are listed in each chart in *italics*.)
2) Next, say to your child: "Find the row where there is a(n) ___. " (These are the question navigation icons listed in the first column. They are underlined.)
3) Then, read the directions to your child. These are in the gray box. Each question type has the same directions for the questions of that question type. The only exception is the Sentence Completion questions on p.90. In the Sentence Completion chart, the directions are in the chart's third column and not in a gray box.

COGAT® QUESTION TYPE 1: PICTURE ANALOGIES (VERBAL SECTION)

Directions for all Picture Analogy questions: Look at these boxes that are on top. The pictures that are inside belong together in some way. Then, look at these boxes that are on the bottom. One of these boxes on the bottom is empty. Look next to the boxes. There is a row of pictures. Which one would go together with this picture that is in the bottom box like these pictures that are in the top boxes?

"Find the row where there is a(n) _____."	Question Number	Answer	Child's Answer
(p. 46) *"Find the page where there is an umbrella at the bottom."* (Help child find the page where questions start.)			
Sun	1	A (person > where person sleeps)	
Fish	2	B (object > 1 part of object)	
Key	3	D (toy version > real version)	
(p. 47) *"Find the page where there is a pair of glasses at the bottom."*			
Car	4	A (similar clothing items; shirts/jackets)	
Spiderweb	5	D (objects > container)	
Truck	6	C (right box has object with similar function, but it is electric)	
(p. 48) *"Find the page where there is a train at the bottom."*			
Star	7	B (shut > open)	
Chair	8	A (plant's habitat > plant)	
Crab	9	C (# of dots on dice = # of wheels on unicycle/car)	
(p. 49) *"Find the page where there is a ball at the bottom."*			
Black Rectangle	10	D (animal's habitat > animal)	
Fork	11	A (object > where object is kept)	
Spoon	12	C (# of shape sides > # of kids)	
(p. 50) *"Find the page where there is a bird at the bottom."*			
Hat	13	A (3D shape > object with this same shape)	
Cup	14	C (something with capacity for many > something with a similar function with capacity for a few)	

Picture Analogy Questions Answered Correctly: _____ out of 14

COGAT® QUESTION TYPE 2: PICTURE CLASSIFICATION (VERBAL SECTION)

Directions for all Picture Classification questions: Look at the top row of pictures. These pictures are alike in a certain way. Then, look at the pictures that are on the bottom row. Which picture that is in the bottom row would go best with the pictures that are in the top row?

"Find the row where there is a(n) _____."	Question Number	Answer	Child's Answer
Heart	15	C (animal homes)	
(p. 51) *"Find the page where there is a house at the bottom."*			
Stoplight	16	A (types of fish)	
Car	17	D (used to cut)	
Key	18	A (odd numbers)	
Boat	19	B (lowercase letters)	
(p. 52) *"Find the page where there is a triangle at the bottom."*			
Sun	20	B (real animals (not toys))	
Chair	21	C (cold weather clothes)	
Arrow	22	D (uppercase consonants)	
Spiderweb	23	A (woodwind instruments)	
(p. 53) *"Find the page where there is a boot at the bottom."*			
Truck	24	C (halves)	

COGAT® QUESTION TYPE 2: PICTURE CLASSIFICATION, CONTINUED (VERBAL SECTION)

"Find the row where there is a(n) _____."	Question Number	Answer	Child's Answer
Shirt	25	A (baby animals)	
Ant	26	B (have shells)	
Chair	27	C (hold liquid)	
(p. 54) *"Find the page where there is a beetle at the bottom."*			
Crab	28	D (hold things together)	
Key	29	C (fruits that grow on trees)	
Butterfly	30	D (animals with stripes)	
Leaf	31	A (live only in water)	

Picture Classification Questions Answered Correctly: _____ out of 17

COGAT® QUESTION TYPE 3: SENTENCE COMPLETION (VERBAL SECTION)

"Find the row where there is a(n)____."	Question Number	Directions (Say to child)	Answer	Child's Answer
(p. 55) *"Find the page where there is a key at the bottom."*				
Tree	32	If you were a biologist, which one would you have at work?	C	
Triangle	33	Which one of these would contain the most seeds?	B	
Shoe	34	In which one of these would water be the deepest?	A	
Duck	35	Which one of these would you see at an appliance store?	D	
(p. 56) *"Find the page where there is a hammer at the bottom."*				
Truck	36	Which one of these would an architect help create?	A	
Crab	37	Which one of these is battery-operated?	B	
Spiderweb	38	If your friend and you were looking at an atlas, which one of these would you most likely see?	C	
Fork	39	Which of these symbols means parking is not allowed?	C	
(p. 57) *"Find the page where there is a leaf at the bottom."*				
Sun	40	Which one of these is a signal?	B	
Spoon	41	Which one of these shows the results of a drought?	D	
Cup	42	Which one of these shows a type of currency?	C	
Chair	43	Which animal would you not see in a polar climate?	B	
(p. 58) *"Find the page where there is a black rectangle at the bottom."*				
Black Star	44	Which one of these is opaque?	C	
Bike	45	Which choice shows a heart at the end, a diamond in the middle, and does not have a rectangle?	C	
Flower	46	Which choice has the letter "S" in between the letter "C" and the letter "T", where the letter "T" is to the right of the letter "S"?	D	
Key	47	Freddie did 3 things tonight: he checked the temperature, played basketball, and ate a salad. What shows all 3 things he used tonight?	D	
(p. 59) *"Find the page where there is a duck at the bottom."*				
Cup	48	Which shows 1 living thing and another non-living thing?	C	
Eye	49	Which shows a triangle in the middle, a circle at the end, and doesn't have a star?	D	
Spoon	50	Which shows these 3 different things: something to wear when it's hot, something to wear when it's cold, and something to use when it's rainy?	B	
Fish	51	Which shows one animal that can both fly and swim and another animal that can not fly, but it can swim.	A	

Sentence Completion Questions Answered Correctly: _____ out of 20

COGAT® QUESTION TYPE 4: NUMBER ANALOGIES (QUANTITATIVE SECTION)

Directions for all Number Analogy questions: Look at these boxes that are on top. The pictures that are inside belong together in some way. Then, look at these boxes that are on the bottom. One of these boxes on the bottom is empty. Look next to the boxes. There is a row of pictures. Which one would go together with this picture that is in the bottom box like these pictures that are in the top boxes?

"Find the row where there is a(n) _____."	Question Number	Answer	Child's Answer
(p. 60) *"Find the page where there is a butterfly at the bottom."*			
Bike	52	C (same)	
Key	53	D (half)	
Crab	54	C (-5)	
(p. 61) *"Find the page where there is a flower at the bottom."*			
Car	55	A (multiply by 3)	

"Find the row where there is a(n) _____."	Question Number	Answer	Child's Answer
Fork	56	B (almost full > just over half)	
Spoon	57	A (2 less sections filled OR # of white and black filled sections reverses)	
(p. 62) *"Find the page where there is a black arrow at the bottom."*			
Star	58	C (multiply by 4)	
Ant	59	C (almost full > empty)	
Crab	60	D (4 items > same 4 items split 2 & 2)	
(p. 63) *"Find the page where there is a shirt at the bottom."*			
Stoplight	61	A (5 items > same 5 items split 2 & 3)	
Pencil	62	A (half)	
Heart	63	C (divide by 4; one-fourth)	

Number Analogies Questions Answered Correctly: _____ out of 12

COGAT® QUESTION TYPE 5: NUMBER SERIES - ABACUS (QUANTITATIVE SECTION)

Directions for all Number Series questions: Here's an abacus. The beads on the first rods have made a pattern. Look at the last rod on the abacus. The beads on this rod are missing. Next to the abacus are four rods. These are the answer choices. Choose which rod would go in the place of the last rod in order to complete the pattern.

"Find the row where there is a(n) _____."	Question Number	Answer	Child's Answer
(p. 64) *"Find the page where there is an eye at the bottom."*			
Triangle	64	C (w/ each rod: -1 bead)	
Cup	65	D (2-4-6-7-6-4)	
Chair	66	B (rods 1,3,5 decrease by 2; 2,4,6 increase by 1)	
Key	67	C (6-6-7-7-4-4)	
(p. 65) *"Find the page where there is a bike at the bottom."*			
Boat	68	A (5-4-3-2-5-4)	
Arrow	69	D (rods 1,3,5,7 decrease by 1; rods 2,4,6 = 1)	
Cup	70	D (rods 1,3,5 increase by 2; 2,4,6 increase by 2)	
Truck	71	C (4-5-3-2-4-5-3)	
(p. 66) *"Find the page where there is a fish at the bottom."*			
Heart	72	D (rods 1,3,5 increase by 1; 2,4,6 decrease by 1)	
Key	73	A (3-5-1-4-3-5)	
Hat	74	B (0-0-7-0-0-7)	
Bug	75	B (beads increase in this pattern: 1, 2, 1, 2, 1, then 2)	
(p. 67) *"Find the page where there is a spoon at the bottom."*			
Plane	76	D (rods 1,3,5,7 increase by 1; 2,4,6 increase by 1)	
Fish	77	A (7-6-5-0-5-6-7)	
Cow	78	C (w/ each rod: +2 beads)	
Car	79	C (beads decrease by 1, by 2, by 1, by 2, etc.)	

Number Series Questions Answered Correctly: _____ out of 16

COGAT® QUESTION TYPE 6: MATH PUZZLES - EQUATIONS (QUANTITATIVE SECTION)

Directions for all Math Puzzles questions: Look at the box that has the question mark. Which number would go here so that both of the sides of this equal sign would have the same amount?

"Find the row with a(n) _____."	Question Number	Answer	Child's Answer	"Find the row with a(n) _____."	Question Number	Answer	Child's Answer
(p. 68) *"Find the page where there is a table at the bottom."*				Spiderweb	90	C	
Pencil	80	C		Truck	91	D	
Star	81	C		Pencil	92	A	
Crab	82	A		Black Rectangle	93	C	
Spiderweb	83	D		(p. 70) *"Find the page where there is a crab at the bottom."*			
Fork	84	D		Heart	94	B	
Spoon	85	A		Ball	95	A	
Shirt	86	B		Train	96	D	
(p. 69) *"Find the page where there is a hand at the bottom."*				Bird	97	C	
Fish	87	A		Stoplight	98	C	
Chair	88	C		House	99	A	
Car	89	A		Shirt	100	A	

COGAT® QUESTION TYPE 6: MATH PUZZLES, CONTINUED (QUANTITATIVE SECTION)

"Find the row with a(n) _____."	Question Number	Answer	Child's Answer	"Find the row with a(n) _____."	Question Number	Answer	Child's Answer
(p. 71) *"Find the page where there is a fork at the bottom."*				(p. 73) *"Find the page where there is a boat at the bottom."*			
Pencil	101	B		Pencil	113	D	
Star	102	D		Star	114	C	
Crab	103	C		Crab	115	D	
Spiderweb	104	D		Spiderweb	116	D	
Fork	105	A		Fork	117	B	
Spoon	106	B		Spoon	118	D	
(p. 72) *"Find the page where there is a cup at the bottom."*							
Heart	107	A					
Ball	108	C					
Train	109	D					
Bird	110	B					
Stoplight	111	D					
House	112	C					

Math Puzzles Questions Answered Correctly: _____ out of 39

COGAT® QUESTION TYPE 7: FIGURE ANALOGIES (NON-VERBAL SECTION)

Directions for all Figure Analogy questions: Look at these boxes that are on top. The pictures that are inside belong together in some way. Then, look at these boxes that are on the bottom. One of these boxes on the bottom is empty. Look next to the boxes. There is a row of pictures. Which one would go together with this picture that is in the bottom box like these pictures that are in the top boxes?

"Find the row where there is a(n) _____."	Question Number	Answer	Child's Answer
(p. 74) *"Find the page where there is an ant at the bottom."*			
Pencil	119	D (rotates 180°, line added in middle)	
Stoplight	120	D (center shape moves to top)	
Crab	121	C (middle shapes align horizontally; color/design from large and small shapes switch)	
(p. 75) *"Find the page where there is a hat at the bottom."*			
Cup	122	C ("x" rotates & shapes inside reverse color)	
Fork	123	B (star becomes hexagon & vice versa, they reverse color; bottom shape reverses color)	
Spoon	124	A (outer shape & center shape switch)	
(p. 76) *"Find the page where there is a wheel at the bottom."*			
Train	125	D (number of dots is the same but white; shape is 3D version of left shape)	
Cup	126	A (large shape turns blue and rotates 180°; stars align horizontally and turn white)	
Chair	127	D (rotates counterclockwise, small shapes reverse color)	
(p. 77) *"Find the page where there is a fish at the bottom."*			
Stoplight	128	B (lines change orientation & in bottom box, separate)	
Boat	129	A (these switch: top left & bottom right; bottom left & top right)	
House	130	C (outer & middle shape switch positions and colors, then align vertically)	

Figure Analogy Questions Answered Correctly: _____ out of 12

COGAT® QUESTION TYPE 8: FIGURE CLASSIFICATION (NON-VERBAL SECTION)

Directions for all Figure Classification questions: Look at the top row of pictures. These pictures are alike in a certain way. Then, look at the pictures that are on the bottom row. Which picture that is in the bottom row would go best with the pictures that are in the top row?

"Find the row where there is a(n) _____."	Question Number	Answer	Child's Answer
(p. 78) *"Find the page where there is a turtle at the bottom."*			
Duck	131	D (divided in half)	
Bug	132	B (rounded edges)	
Crab	133	A (diamond in middle)	
Spiderweb	134	A (shapes & small circles are opposite colors)	